WINDOW, CASTLE ASHBY, NORTHAMPTONSHIRE

A

GLOSSARY OF TERMS

USED IN

GRECIAN, ROMAN, ITALIAN,

AND

Gothic Architecture.

THE FIFTH EDITION, ENLARGED.

EXEMPLIFIED BY SEVENTEEN HUNDRED WOODCUTS.

VOL. II. PLATES. PART I.

OXFORD,

JOHN HENRY PARKER;

DAVID BOGUE, FLEET STREET, LONDON.

M DCCC L.

OXFORD :
PRINTED BY I. SHRIMPTON.

DESCRIPTIVE INDEX OF THE ILLUSTRATIONS.

b

ABACUS.

PERPENDICULAR. Croydon, Surrey, c. 1450. Henry
VIIth's chapel, Westminster, A.D. 1503 . . — 1

ACANTHUS . . . . . . 6 —

ACROTERIA . . . . . . 6 —

ALMERY, or AMBRY, or LOCKER. Chapel in Chepstow
castle. Bramshot, Hampshire . . . 10 —

AMBRY. Foulis, Perthshire, Scotland . . . — 3

The Gothic architecture of Scotland differs so much from that
of England, and has at present been so little investigated, that it is
hardly safe to assign a date to any particular work by comparison.
The present rich and beautiful specimen may, however, be safely
assigned to the beginning of the sixteenth century, its character is much
more like the French Flamboyant than the English Perpendicular,
though partaking in some degree of both.

· Rushden, Northamptonshire . . . — 3

This occurs in good Decorated work of about the middle of the
fourteenth century, it is chiefly remarkable for having retained the
wooden door, and having within the small niche for the cruets of
the altar.

Lincoln cathedral . . . . . — 3

From one of the chapels in the south transept, part of the original
work, and therefore according to the history belonging to the time of
S. Hugh, or about A.D. 1200, a very early date for such pure and good
Early English work, but the history of the church is perfectly clear
and well authenticated, and it only proves that the progress of art at
that period was more rapid than has been commonly supposed, and
that it advanced more rapidly in some places than in others. It is not
usual to find such good work quite so early.

Drayton, Berkshire . . . . . 292 —

This example retains its old oak doors with the original ironwork;
these are very rarely met with, but either part of the hinges, or traces
of them, generally remain, and the rabbet, or rebate, in the stone for
receiving the doors, often serves to distinguish the Ambry from any
other kind of recess in the wall. In the example from Bramshot both
the rabbet and the hooks of the hinges are very distinctly shewn.

ALTAR . . . . 13 —

An altar complete with its hangings, distinguished as the reredos,
(upper frontal, or retrofrontal) curtains, and lower frontal, (or antepen-
dium,) with the fringed frontlet on its upper border. The host is sus-
pended above, and a prayer-stool is placed in front. This engraving is
a fac-simile from an illumination in a manuscript of Lydgate's life of
S. Edmund, in the British Museum, Harl., 2278. The object of giving
this specimen is to shew the manner in which the plain stone altars
were ornamented (or vested) at the time they were erected.

	PAGE	PLATE

ARCH.

S. Mary le Wigford, Lincoln, c. 1200 . . — 17

This is evidently an imitation of the cathedral, but probably rather later.

Nave, Lincoln cathedral, c. 1220 — ib.

Another example of a plain Early English arch from Barton Stacey, Wiltshire, is here added to shew a very common type in country churches.

DECORATED. Chipping Wardon, Northamptonshire, c. 1350. Howden, Yorkshire, c. 1350 . — 18

Early English. Barton Stacey, Wiltshire.

Dorchester, Oxfordshire, circa 1300 . . . — 19

PERPENDICULAR, with shafts, nave of S. Mary's, Oxford, c. 1488. Panelled, Sherborne, Dorsetshire, A.D. 1490 — 20

Minster Lovell, Oxfordshire, c. 1430 . . — ib.

These are the tower-arches in the centre of the church, the arrangement is very peculiar, and very elegant, and is believed to be unique.

ARCH-BUTTRESS. Hartlepool, Durham. (See BUTTRESS.) 46 —

ASTRAGAL . . . . . . 49 —

BALISTRARIA. (See LOOPHOLE, or OILLET) . . 52 —

BALL-FLOWER . . . . . . 53 —

Stringcourse, Kiddington, Oxon, c. 1350. Tabernacle, Exeter cathedral, A.D. 1290. Doorway, Bloxham, Oxon, c. 1280. Doorway, Chipping-Norton, Oxon, c. 1320. Monument, Oxford cathedral, c. 1300. Window, Gloucester cathedral, A.D. 1320. Spire, Salisbury cathedral, two examples, c. 1300. Window-jamb, Oxford cathedral, c. 1320 . . . — 21

The object of this plate is to shew the various modes in which this favourite ornament was applied during the period of its prevalence, the

Notre dame la riche, Tours.

The grounds on which this early date is assigned have been already mentioned : this is a very fine example of pure Early English work, and early in the style, though the date is earlier than it is usual to find such work. It exhibits part of the north aisle and clerestory of the choir, and part of the transept. The buttresses are of two kinds, small ones between the windows and large ones which divide the bays. The lesser ones have a chamfer for the greater part of their length, and which is finished with a capital, but in the large ones the chamfer is very wide and occupies nearly the whole depth of the buttress, and is also finished with a capital. The face of the buttress is by this considerably narrowed, it is deeply moulded and has in the centre a banded shaft with capital and base, and at each angle is placed a detached shaft similar to the centre one, but more slender. The capitals of these three shafts combine with that of the chamfer, thus carrying out the same idea as in the pillars of the choir where the capitals of the small shafts are combined with that of the centre pillars, as shewn in plate 50. The pediment or capping of the buttress is plain and very massive, to support the arch or flying buttress which connects it with the clerestory.

The chamfer is finished in a simple and elegant manner by a trefoil.

This is chamfered, and is finished with a pediment or gablet.

Termination of chamfer of
buttress, Higham Ferrars.

	PAGE	PLATE

CAPITALS (and ENTABLATURES). GRECIAN DORIC.
    ROMAN DORIC. GRECIAN IONIC. ROMAN IONIC.
    CORINTHIAN. COMPOSITE . . .   —   44

    NORMAN. White tower, London, c. 1080 . .   —   45

This is one of the capitals of the chapel in the Tower of London which was built by Gundulph, bishop of Rochester, in 1081. It is a very valuable example as exhibiting the peculiarities of the early Norman capitals. The general design of them seems to have been an imitation, though sometimes extremely rude, of the Corinthian capital; they have almost invariably the volute at the angles, and in some instances, as in some of those in the White tower, have a row of short stiff leaves in imitation of the foliage below. There is also another peculiar feature which is very characteristic of this early style, this is the plain projection which occupies the place of the central branches of the caulicoli, and is in general either left square, as at Caen, or cut into the form of the tau cross, as in this instance. Capitals of this form occur in the work of Remigius at Lincoln, in the early portion of the crypt at Canterbury, and in the crypt at Oxford castle.

    S. Nicholas, Caen, c. 1100 . . . .   —   ib.

This is of the same general design as the last, but a little varied.

    Whitby parish church, c. 1100 . . . .   —   ib.

In this a further deviation has taken place, the projection being cut into a kind of lozenge.

    Westminster hall, c. 1090 . . . .   —   ib.

This occurs in the oldest part of Westminster hall, which was built by William Rufus.

    Lincoln cathedral, c. 1100 . . . .   —   ib.

This singular capital occurs in the west front of the cathedral in the portion built by Remigius in the reign of William I. The foliage is very remarkable, and might at first sight be taken to be of much later date, but a little examination will shew it to be very different, and on comparison with some of the capitals in the White tower, it will be found that the foliage is the same in character but different in proportion. The mid-rib of the leaves at the angles is detached and forms a kind of loop. The arched moulding shewn in this example is of early Norman character. The rest of the capitals in the work of Remigius are similar to those described under White tower.

    Crypt, Canterbury, c. 1100 . . . .   —   ib.

This belongs to the earlier portion of the crypt. This crypt under the choir is part of the work of Ernulf soon after 1100, but the sculpture of the capitals has evidently been executed after they were erected, and

CAPITALS.

Capital and Base, North Transept, Winchester Cathedral.

	PAGE	PLATE

may have been done at intervals when convenient, some of them are still unfinished (see BOAST), this work having probably been interrupted by the great fire and never resumed.

Waterperry, Oxfordshire, c. 1180 — 46

This is a very common form of Norman capitals, and seems to have been in use at almost all periods.

Cassington, Oxfordshire 108 —

Is a good specimen of the common cushion capital. Another variety of this form is also here given but of earlier date.

Dorchester, Oxfordshire, c. 1180 — ib.

This is taken from the original chancel-arch. It is very peculiar in its form, and its foliage is of rather late character.

Steetley, Derbyshire . ib. —

Is from a small and interesting church of pure Norman work

Gloucester cathedral . . . . . ib. —

S. Peter's, Northampton, c. 1160 or earlier . . — ib.

This is one of the finest examples of a rich Norman church in the kingdom. The specimen here given is from the chancel-arch. It exhibits besides the capitals, which are of the same general form as Waterperry, the interlaced and beaded ornaments of the shafts. From the similarity of ornaments with those on the work of Bishop Alexander at Lincoln, it may be of the same date, c. 1140.

Grafton Underwood, Northamptonshire, c. 1180 . — ib.

The foliage is of rather late character.

Haseley, Oxfordshire, c. 1200 . . . . — ib.

The mouldings of the arch and the foliage shew this to be of transition character.

CAPITALS.	PAGE	PLATE
Easton, Hampshire	108	—

This is of late or transition character.

NORMAN ; ENGLISH TRANSITION.

The capitals of this period frequently display great richness in their foliage, which partakes both of the Norman and Early English cha-racter.

	PAGE	PLATE
Christ Church cathedral, Oxford, c. 1180 (two examples)	—	47

The first example is taken from the south aisle of the choir, and shews a combination of a capital and two corbels, the latter supporting the diagonal ribs of the vaulting. The second is from one of the pillars of the nave ; the foliage creeping up upon the abacus is a very unusual feature, it is quite of transition character.

	PAGE	PLATE
Canterbury cathedral, A.D. 1177	—	ib.

This is from the choir, and is the work of William of Sens. The foliage is a close imitation of Corinthian.

	PAGE	PLATE
Oakham castle, Rutlandshire, c. 1180 . . .	—	ib.

The building from which this is taken, the hall, the only part now remaining of the ancient castle, is a very interesting one. The design and execution of the ornamental parts are particularly fine and good. In the capital here given, the foliage and volutes, and even the caulicoli of the Corinthian, are closely imitated, but the tooth-ornament which was then just coming into use is introduced into the bell, and on the arch, while the abacus has a Norman ornament. This combination very clearly points out its transition character and its date.

	PAGE	PLATE
Foreign examples of TRANSITION. Murrhard, c. 1188 .	—	48
Soissons, choir, A.D. 1212	—	ib.

There is much resemblance between this and Canterbury. The upper moulding of the bell is ornamented with the nail-head instead of the tooth-ornament as at Oakham, this ornament never having come into such general use in France.

	PAGE	PLATE
S. Nicolas, Blois, c. 1200 (two examples.) . .	—	ib.

This church is of particular interest from its connection with Lincoln cathedral, the architect of the latter having been a native of Blois, and there are many curious points of resemblance in the details of the two churches, especially the plate tracery of circular windows.

	PAGE	PLATE
EARLY ENGLISH. Burton Latimer, Northamptonshire, c. 1190	—	49

The square section of the upper member of the abacus shews its early character, partaking of Norman, and marks it as belonging to the period of transition, and therefore probably rather before A.D. 1200.

CAPITALS.

ABBEY OF JUMIÈGES, NORMANDY.

Jumieges.

In the ruins of the abbey of Jumièges in Normandy there are several capitals ornamented with foliage painted on a plain surface; this painting is clearly of Norman character and date, and as the foundation of the abbey is known to be early, they have long been supposed to be of that period: (the church was consecrated in 1067.) But it has recently been discovered by accident that this painting is executed on plaster, and that under the plaster is some rude and early sculpture, similar to other early Norman capitals as already described; the painting is therefore of *late* Norman date, and it agrees much better with the character of late Norman sculpture than with the early date to which it has been usually assigned.

	PAGE	PLATE
Bloxham, Oxfordshire, c. 1190	—	49

The same may be said of this as of Burton Latimer.

Woodford, Northamptonshire, c. 1190 . . .	—	ib.

In this the foliage has a more decided Early English character, but the abacus still partakes of the Norman.

Haseley, Oxfordshire, c. 1200	109	—

This, though one of the capitals of an Early English door, has some Norman character about it which shews its early date.

Nun Monkton, Yorkshire, c. 1200 . . .	110	—

This is from a window of a very curious little church, and is of early date. The abacus is square in section, but is indented on the lower edge, which gives it a very singular appearance. The dripstone shews the nail-head, and the chamfer is filled with tooth-ornaments.

Hereford cathedral, c. 1200	109	—

This beautiful and early example of the capital of a small shaft has the nail-head and tooth-ornament on its mouldings.

EARLY ENGLISH. Lincoln cathedral, choir, c. 1200 .	—	50

This portion of the cathedral is one of the earliest, as it is also one of the most beautiful specimens of this style which we possess. The foliage throughout is marked by the greatest boldness and freedom, and

CAPITALS.   PAGE   PLATE

in the example here given the combination of the capitals of the slender
detached shafts with that of the solid pillar in the centre is highly inge-
nious and beautiful, the abacus of the capital serving at the same time
as a band to the vaulting shaft which is carried through without any
other ornament.

S. Mary le Wigford, Lincoln, c. 1200   .   .   .   —   50

This is the same in general design, and has evidently been copied from
those in the choir of the cathedral, but the abacus is different in form.

Another example from a window-jamb in the same
church   110   —

Rushden, Northamptonshire   109   —

A small example from the sedilia, of the same character as the last.

Naseby, Northamptonshire, c. 1220   .   .   .   —   49

This is of later character; the introduction of heads among the foliage
was used occasionally both in this and the succeeding styles.

Desborough, Northamptonshire, c. 1220   .   .   —   50

This is of early date, and
is strong and massive in its
form, but is a good specimen
of the style as found in country
churches.

COGENHOE, NORTHANTS.

Another curious example is
here introduced from Cogenhoe, as besides its singular
character, it is a specimen of
the early introduction of armo-
rial bearings in this situation,
the arms being those of Sir
Nicholas de Cogenhoe, the
founder of the church, who
died in the time of Edward I.
See Bridges' Northampton-

O. JEWITT, delt. sc.

Cogenhoe, Northamptonshire.

shire, vol. i. p. 349.   It is also an early instance of the introduction
of heads as part of the ornament of the capital, which is more frequent
in Decorated work, though occasionally found in Norman.

Lincoln cathedral, Presbytery, c. 1260   .   .   .   —   ib.

This belongs to a later period, but is equally beautiful; nothing can
exceed the grace and elegance of the foliage in this portion of the
building. The shafts in the example given are relieved and ornamented
by small knots of foliage rising from the centre shaft, and partly over-
lying the detached ones.

CAPITALS.

Presbytery, Lincoln.

The greatest variety of design occurs in the capitals of this building, and an additional example is here introduced to illustrate another form of foliage.

There is no mistaking the decided Early English character of this foliage, and of the other details of the Presbytery of Lincoln, although the windows have bar-tracery, which is considered, in one sense, as marking the commencement of the Decorated style.

Warmington, Northants., c. 1280 (two examples) . — 49

These capitals support the wooden groined roof of the beautiful church to which they belong. It is rather late in the style, but all its details are worth studying; perhaps 1260 would be a more correct date than the one given in the plate. A set of drawings of this church has been lately published by Mr. Caveler.

DECORATED. **Hampton Poyle, Oxfordshire, c. 1300** . — 51

This curious example is early in the style, and belongs to the geometrical period, of which the east window of the church is a good specimen.

Harrington, Northamptonshire, c. 1300.

Another capital from the same church . 110 —

Cottingham, Nottinghamshire . 111 —

Is an example of similar character to the first from Hampton Poyle.

Harrington, Northamptonshire, circa 1300.

The example here given is of the same early period, but is singular from the character of its foliage, which runs round the bell in the manner of a wreath. The other capitals in the church have the oak and vine leaves.

CAPITALS.

Christ Church, York.

Shewing the varieties of Decorated foliage.

Christ Church, York.

A corbel for carrying the arch mouldings is combined with this capital in a similar manner to one of those on Plate 99. It is also singular in having no neck-mould.

Dorchester, Oxfordshire, c. 1300 . .

This is a good plain example without any thing peculiar, though probably of somewhat later date than here assigned to it.

Beverley minster, circa 1320. (Two examples) . . .

	PAGE	PLATE
	—	51
	—	ib.

Sandhurst, Kent . . . . . 110 | —

A good example of a form of very general occurrence.

Lincoln cathedral, c. 1360 (misprinted 1300) . . | — | ib.

This capital is from the interior of the west end, and though of good Decorated character itself, the work in which it occurs is of transition from Decorated to Perpendicular.

Southwell minster, Notts, c. 1300 . . . | — | ib.

This is taken from the very beautiful screen at the entrance of the choir, all the details of which are exquisitely fine.

PERPENDICULAR. Wellingborough, Northants., c. 1450 . | — | 52

This is a very good and characteristic example of a plain capital. It occurs in the chancel.

Newark, Nottinghamshire, c. 1380 . . . | — | ib.

This is one of the capitals of the nave, which are all of similar character, and are very unusual.

Stoke in Teignhead, Devonshire, c. 1480 . . | — | ib.

This shews a peculiarity which is of frequent occurrence in the Perpendicular of Devonshire, that is, the abacus instead of overhanging as usual, recedes and allows the greatest projection to the foliage, which thus appears more like a band than a capital.

	PAGE	PLATE
CORBELS.		
York cathedral, c. 1450　.　.　.　.　.　.	—	61

Two additional examples are here introduced.

Polebrook, c. 1200.

This gives also another variety of the chamfer termination, and a mask.

| Norwich cathedral　. | 143 | — |

This represents a hart lying in the water, and is intended as a rebus of Walter Lyhart, the bishop by whom this part of the cathedral was built.

CORBEL - TABLES.

| NORMAN. Romsey church, Hants, c. 1180　.　. | — | 62 |
| EARLY ENGLISH. Romsey, Hants, c. 1220　.　. | — | ib. |

In this example the corbel with the tooth-ornament is regularly alternate with the others; it is taken from the north side of the church, but the head is brought from another situation for the sake of variety.

| Portsmouth, c. 1230, or rather earlier probably　.　. | — | ib. |

In this example the corbels are all taken from the south side of the church, though not in the exact order here represented. The church was begun about 1180, but probably not finished until after 1200.

Polebrook, Northamptonshire.

Lincoln.

This date is probably rather too early, the exact age of this very beautiful tower and spire is not known, but must be about 1300.

This has been removed from its original position in the north-east corner within a few years. The mark of it in the plaster is still visible.

This is from the large piers of the choir, and is there used on the central pillar between the slender detached shafts. See Plate 150.

This is an ornament used in one of the mouldings of the chapter-house door, but in form and character it corresponds very closely with an Early English crocket.

DECORATED STYLE.

DENTELS . . . . 165 —

DIAPER. Two examples. Tomb of William de Valence,
  Westminster abbey . . . . . ib. —

DOORWAYS. Supposed SAXON. Brixworth, Northants . 175 —

 NORMAN. Essendine chapel, Rutland, c. 1130 . . — 71

  S. Margaret's at Cliffe, near Dover, Kent, c. 1130 . — ib.

  S. Ebbe's, Oxford, c. 1140 . . . . — 72

   This church is modern, but this old doorway has been preserved and
rebuilt in the wall of the vestry.

  Iffley, Oxfordshire, c. 1140 . . . . — ib.

   Or more probably 1160. See the grounds for this date in Archæolog.
Journal, vol. iv. p. 219.

  Fordington, near Dorchester, Dorsetshire, c. 1160 . — 73

   This is a very curious example. The sculptures have evidently

DOORWAYS.

been cut after the door was built, and appear to have been drawn on the surface, and only so much of it cut away as would give relief to the figures. The kite-shaped shields and nasals shew sufficiently its Norman date.

	PAGE	PLATE
Stoneleigh, Warwickshire, c. 1160 . . .	—	73
Penmon, Anglesea	—	74

The Welsh antiquaries are generally inclined to assign a very early date to this and similar examples. The probability however seems to be that they are more likely to be later than earlier than corresponding examples in England. The very thick abacus is often a mark of early work, but it is also frequently only a sign of rude country work, or a provincialism. It is difficult to find a dated example of stone sculpture in this country before the twelfth century, to which period the Norman doorways with sculpture in the head almost invariably belong.

	PAGE	PLATE
Barton Seagrave, Northamptonshire, c. 1150 . .	—	ib.
Middleton Stoney, Oxfordshire, c. 1150 . .	—	ib.
Dorchester, Oxfordshire, c. 1160 . . .	—	ib.

This doorway is very late Norman, almost of transition character; the head of it affords a good example of reticulated masonry, which is not very common in England.

	PAGE	PLATE
Fritwell, Oxfordshire, c. 1150. Kirkham priory, Yorkshire, c. 1150. Newington, Oxfordshire, c. 1160 .	—	75
Cuddesden, Oxfordshire, c. 1160 . . .	—	ib.

This is quite of transitional character, the lozenge moulding with the points projecting and standing clear app~~roac~~hes very near to the tooth-ornament; the capitals are more E~~arl~~y English than Norman. The door retains its original iron ~~wo~~rk. For the mouldings see . .

	PAGE	PLATE
	—	120
Chapter-house, Oxford, c. 1160 . . .	176	—
Nail-heads on door, Compton, Berks . . .	177	—

EARLY ENGLISH. Lutton, Huntingdonshire, c. 1200 . — 76

This form is to be found in all the styles, but most frequently in the Early English. (See note, p. 43, vol. i.)

	PAGE	PLATE
Burton Latimer, Northamptonshire, c. 1220 . .	—	ib.
Warmington, Northamptonshire, c. 1260 . .	—	ib.
Kidlington, Oxfordshire, c. 1220 . . .	—	77

The square form and the mouldings of the abacus mark this as early in the style.

	PAGE	PLATE
Irchester, Northamptonshire, c. 1220 . .	—	ib.

An example of the use of stones of different colours, for the sake of

EARLY ENGLISH STYLE.

	PAGE	PLATE
FLUTINGS or FLUTES. Grecian Doric. Parthenon	211	—
Grecian Ionic. Erectheum, and cabled flutes	ib.	—
FOIL-ARCH. Trefoil opening. Trefoil arches. Cinquefoil arch	ib.	—
FONT. Norman. Coleshill, Warwickshire, c. 1150	—	89

Arcade from do., see Plate 8.

This is a very curious and remarkable example, and is valuable for the arcade filled with rich foliage with which it is surrounded, part of which is given under ARCADE, and the rest here. The form of the nimbus is remarkable.

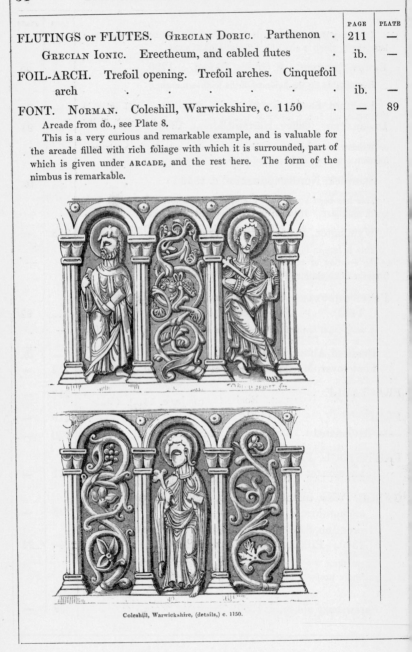

Coleshill, Warwickshire, (details,) c. 1150.

	PAGE	PLATE
FONT.		
It is only the bowl which is Norman, and it has been placed on a later shaft, which is also of a different kind of stone.		
EARLY ENGLISH. S. Giles's, Oxford, c. 1220. . .	—	90
Remarkable for the boldness of the tooth-ornament.		
Lackford, Sussex, c. 1250	—	ib.
DECORATED. Offley, Hertfordshire, c. 1350 . .	—	91
Window tracery either of the whole window or only the head was a frequent ornament of Decorated fonts.		
Stanwick, Northamptonshire, c. 1350 . . .	—	ib.
This has been a very rich example, but has lost its shaft and been much mutilated. It stands in a very interesting church.		
Wymington, Bedfordshire, c. 1380 . .	213	—
This is late in the style and is from a remarkable church, the date of the erection of which is tolerably well ascertained. See a pillar from the same church, Pl. 148; part of the roof, p. 399.		
PERPENDICULAR. Fotheringhay, Northamptonshire, A.D. 1440	—	92
A very usual form of a Perpendicular font.		
Bradford Abbas, Dorsetshire, c. 1480 . . .	—	ib.
Font cover, Monksilver, Somersetshire . . .	212	—
FRACTABLE	217	—
FRET	219	—
—— Reticulated	220	—
FRITHSTOOL, FRIDSTOOL, or FREEDSTOOL. Beverley minster	221	—
GABLE. West end of Bede-house, Higham Ferrars, Northamptonshire	223	—
George Inn, Salisbury, c 1320 or 1350. Salisbury, A.D. 1360. Eltham palace, Kent, c. 1490 . .	—	93
These three are all examples of the gables of timber houses, and might more properly perhaps have been called Barge-boards, which see.		
Shrewsbury abbey, c. 1350. Newgate, York . .	59	—

East Dereham.

	PAGE	PLATE
HIP-KNOB. Friar gate, Derby	254	—
See also Plate 86.		
HOODMOULD TERMINATIONS. NORMAN. Malmsbury abbey, Wilts, c. 1150	—	98
This is a very characteristic ornament, and is of frequent occurrence in Norman work.		
EARLY ENGLISH. S. Benedict's, Lincoln, c. 1250 .	—	ib.
Stanwick, Northamptonshire, c. 1230 . .	—	ib.
Garsington, Oxfordshire, c. 1200 . . .	—	ib.
DECORATED. Merton college chapel, Oxford, A.D. 1277 .	—	ib.
This appears to be the head of Edward I., in whose reign the chapel was built.		
Rushden, Northamptonshire	—	ib.
PERPENDICULAR. Chippenham, Wilts, c. 1460. Layer Marney, Essex, c. 1520	—	ib.
Marston, Oxfordshire, c. 1520	—	ib.
This contains the monogram MARIA, so frequently used.		
HOUR-GLASS STAND. Leigh church, Kent . .	255	—
IMPOST. CONTINUOUS. Fig. A. S. Pierre, Avignon .	259	—
Finchale priory, Durham, A.D. 1266, the second example	—	99
Keyingham	—	100
DISCONTINUOUS. Fig. B. La Chapelle, Brussels .	ib.	—
Finchale priory, first example . . .	—	99
S. Nicholas, Coutances, c. 1250 . . .	—	ib.
Cathedral, S. Lo, Normandy, c. 1300 . . .	—	ib.
SHAFTED. Fig. C	ib.	—
BANDED. Fig. D. Lucca cathedral . . .	ib.	—
DISCONTINUOUS and BANDED. Dreux, Normandy .	260	—
DISCONTINUOUS and SHAFTED. Lowick, Northamptonshire	—	100
CONTINUOUS and SHAFTED alternately. Yarmouth, Norfolk. Ely cathedral	—	ib.

	PAGE	PLATE
IMPOST.		
CONTINUOUS and DISCONTINUOUS. S. Crux, York .	—	99

This is very curious. The annexed plan, in which A shews the pier and B the arch mouldings, will explain the junction of the two suites of mouldings more clearly.

	PAGE	PLATE
S. Helen's, Stonegate, York .	—	ib.

This is partly continuous, but the outer mouldings are carried on a corbel.

	PAGE	PLATE
IONIC ORDER. Capital from the Erectheum, Athens .	267	—

A

B

Section of pillar and arch-mouldings.

	PAGE	PLATE
IRON-WORK. Part of a door, Winchester cathedral .	—	100*

N.B. The woodcut is turned so as to place the top of the figure on the left hand.

	PAGE	PLATE
Monument of Queen Eleanor, Westminster abbey, A.D. 1294	—	ib.

A very fine example of that period, very similar in character to that on the chapter-house door, York.

	PAGE	PLATE
On an Early English chest	125	—
Iron coffer	137	—
Nail-heads. On a Norman door . . .	177	—
On a Decorated door	181	—
Of Early English hinges . . p. 179 and	253	—
Escutcheons on doors . . p. 198 and	199	—
Hour-glass stand	255	—
CRAMP, Westminster abbey . . .	269	—
Nail-head. Henry VII.'s chapel . . .	ib.	—
Cathedral, and S. Martin, Laon . . .	ib.	—

Lettern, Lingfield, Surrey.

This with its screen occupies the last bay of the south aisle of the choir at its junction with the eastern transept. The fire-place belonging to it is inserted in the Early English arcade, and the original chimney still remains on the outside.

In this instance there are two lavatories adjoining, and they are of fifteenth century date, and have been inserted with their niches and panelling, under the Decorated arches of the cloisters.

A curious and early example, and may probably be somewhat earlier than the date here given.

The book is chained to the desk as mentioned in the text.

  A very plain and rather singular example of the revived use of the
lettern in the time of Charles II.   It formed part of the furniture of
the chancel built by Dr. South.   The book of Homilies is placed upon
it, and it may have been originally intended for that purpose, according
to the Injunctions.

Albury, Hertfordshire.   Islip, Oxfordshire.

This is an early example of the billet moulding, as the castle was built by order of Robert, duke of Normandy. The mouldings are very simple.

This is the section of an arch at the west end, which was the work of Remigius the first bishop. The ornament under the dripstone is very characteristic of early work.

The ornaments of this, the flat billet and sunk lozenge, which are shallow and require little skill in the execution, bespeak the early character of this example. This is the work of Ernulph.

A good example of plain Norman.

This is from the work of William of Sens, and a comparison of this with the one above it, which is from the same part of the cathedral but of later date, will shew the progress which had been made between the two periods. In the first the work is of the most simple design and the work shallow, while in the last a more elegant outline has been given, and the cutting is bold, deep, and finished. See Willis's Canterbury, p. 88.

The keeled moulding on the angle of this shews a late date, and a tendency to transition.

This building, which is commonly called John of Gaunt's stables, has a fine entrance gateway, of which this is a section. It is remarkable

MOULDINGS.   PAGE   PLATE

on several accounts, first the sunk roses or flowers on the dripstone;
secondly, the ornament in the hollow, which, at first sight, closely re-
sembles the tooth-ornament, but differs from it in several respects, and
particularly in its want of projection, the angles formed by the sides
being very obtuse and the centre flat. The same ornament occurs in
the west doorway of the cathedral, which was the work of Bishop Alexander about 1140. The next peculiarity is the moulding which occurs
twice in the section. This is a round with a groove or channel taken
out on its most projecting part.

S. Peter's, Northampton, c. 1140; arch on the tower .   —   112

The section here given is that of an arch on the exterior of the west
side of the tower, the original intention of which does not seem to have
been well understood. It is, however, most probable that it was the
arch of the original west window. The church is a celebrated example,
and this arch will fully bear out its reputation. The details are extremely beautiful and varied, and worked with great delicacy but not
much depth.

Window, Moyes's hall, Bury S. Edmund's, c. 1160 .   —   ib.

Door, Middleton Stoney, Oxfordshire, c. 1160 .   .   —   ib.

Ambrosden, Oxfordshire, c. 1160   .   .   —   ib.

These are all good specimens of late Norman work.

MOULDINGS and ORNAMENTS. Early NORMAN .   —   113

These examples are brought together for the purpose of shewing
what were the general modes by which ornament was produced in the
early Norman buildings. It will be seen that this was in general ac-
complished by making the simplest forms possible, two sets of oblique
lines crossing each other, and then from the centres of the lozenges
thus formed cutting away the stone slopingly to the points, and thus
by lowering one set giving relief to the alternate ones. By these means
the lozenges at Old Sarum, Deeping, and Walmer, and the hatchings
at Westminster, have been produced.

White tower, tower of London, A.D. 1081   .   .   —   ib.

This is the abacus of the capital described on Plate 45. The ornament consists of the cable, and a variety of what is sometimes called
star moulding. This is formed by drawing the diagonals of a square
and cutting down the intervals.

Clemping, Sussex, c. 1100   .   .   .   —   ib.

This ornament consists merely of a set of hollow squares which have
been cut down in the manner above described.

	PAGE	PLATE

MOULDINGS AND ORNAMENTS.

Remains of Old Sarum. In the wall of the north gate of the Close, Salisbury, c. 1120 . . . . — 113

In the walls of the Close and in some of the interior walls of the cathedral at Salisbury, are built in many stones carved with Norman details, some of early and some of later date. These must evidently have been brought from the cathedral of Old Sarum when it was pulled down and the present structure built. The specimens here given are from the north gate of the Close, and from the character of their ornaments have evidently belonged to the older portions of the ancient cathedral.

Deeping S. James, Lincolnshire, c. 1120 . . — ib.

This shews a raised lozenge, and single zig-zag.

Walmer, Kent, c. 1120 . . . . — ib.

Has the sunk lozenge and double billet.

Transept, Winchester cathedral, A.D. 1090 . . — ib.

This has been called a prismatic billet. It is produced by marking out squares on the three sides of the moulding, and cutting away the alternate spaces, and has much the effect of bricks set end-ways and corner-ways.

Westminster hall, A.D. 1097 . . . . — ib.

This is called the hatched or saw-tooth ornament; it is here worked on the three faces of the string.

Southwell minster, Nottinghamshire, c. 1100 . . — ib.

The first of these is an arch-moulding, and shews the ornament mentioned before, and also a singular one of double cones or fusils lying side by side, and which produce a curious effect. The second is an ornament on a capital.

NORMAN. *Zigzag* or *chevron* . . . . — 114

This Plate presents an assemblage of varieties of the zigzag, the most characteristic ornament of the Norman period. See also pp. 128 and 525 —

North Hinksey, Berks . . . . . — ib.

This is a common form; the mouldings consist of a hollow and a round cut on the plane of the wall.

Guibray, Normandy . . . . . — ib.

Shews the zigzag projecting, that is, cut with salient and re-entering angles.

Fresne, Camilly, Normandy . . . . — ib.

Has the two varieties forming a hollow lozenge between.

	PAGE	PLATE
MOULDINGS AND ORNAMENTS.		
Bredgar, Kent	—	114

Has the nail-head on two of the mouldings.

West door, Lincoln cathedral, c. 1140 . . . — ib.

This is from the elaborate work of Bishop Alexander, in the time of Stephen, and is remarkable for exhibiting an ornament very similar to, though not identical with, the ball-flower, and another which was afterwards used in Early English work. Very similar ornaments occur in France, in late Norman work, as at Notre Dame, Paris.

New Romney, Kent . . . . . — ib.

Shews another variety of the projecting zigzag.

Iffley, Oxfordshire . . . . . — ib.

A series cut on a plain surface.

Hadiscoe, Norfolk . . . . . — ib.

This is a very singular example, the zigzag being reversed and cut across the moulding.

Andover, Hants . . . . . — ib.

Combined with the scallop.

Beaulieu, near Caen, Normandy . . . — ib.

Is an example of the mode of filling up the zigzag in rich work.

Barfreston, Kent . . . . . — ib.

Is a very curious example. It is cut on two planes, that on the lower one forming a regular zigzag, while that on the upper is interrupted, and forms alternate lozenges with the lower one.

Sutterton, Lincolnshire . . . . — ib.

Shews a very good but unusual mode of ornamenting the zigzag.

Cable. **Romsey, Hants** . . . . — 115

This moulding is used in almost all periods of Norman work.

Twining stem. **Wimboltsham, Norfolk** . . — ib.

This is another variety of the same, but not so common.

1. *Beaded,* 2. *Twisted panel.* **Durham cathedral** . — ib.

Is an unusual variety of the same type.

Billeted cable. **Jew's House, Lincoln** . . — ib.

Is another variety, but ornamented with the billet.

Intersecting and cable. **S. Georges de Boscherville** . — ib.

MOULDINGS AND ORNAMENTS.

	PAGE	PLATE
Nail-head. Upton S. Leonard's, Gloucestershire .	—	115

The nail-head being an ornament easily cut, was much used in almost all periods of Norman work, and also in the earlier examples of Early English capitals, &c., and may be safely considered as the origin of the tooth ornament.

	PAGE	PLATE
S. Contet, near Caen, Normandy . . .	—	ib.

This and another of similar character are generally used in late or transition work, as at Glastonbury abbey, and at Hargrave, Plate 120.

	PAGE	PLATE
Star. Herringfleet, Suffolk	—	ib.

This ornament, which is formed by cutting down in a sloping manner the intervals between a square and its diagonals, is much used in abaci and similar situations.

	PAGE	PLATE
Lozenge. Tickencote, Rutland . . .	—	ib.

This church has a very rich chancel-arch, from which this moulding is taken. The lozenge is formed by the junction of two zigzags.

	PAGE	PLATE
Enriched Lozenge. Montivilliers, Normandy . .	—	ib.

In this the spaces in the lozenges are merely sunk.

	PAGE	PLATE
Segmental Billet. Abbaye aux Dames, Caen . .	—	116
Nebule and Billet. S. Contet-les-Caen . .	—	ib.
Roll Billet, double. Binham Priory, Norfolk . .	—	ib.
Square Billet, double. S. Augustine's, Canterbury .	—	ib.
Segmental and square Billet. S. Mary's, Leicester .	—	ib.
Billet and studded. Llandaff cathedral . .	—	ib.

The billet in its various forms being merely the retaining or cutting away of alternate portions of any given moulding, was an ornament easily executed, and therefore extensively used in all periods of Norman work. In the Abbaye aux Dames it is a half round laid on the flat faces of a three-sided moulding. In S. Contet, Binham, and Llandaff, it is cut on round mouldings, at S. Augustine's on a square, and at S. Mary's, Leicester, is alternately a half round and half square.

	PAGE	PLATE
Cloisters, Peterborough cathedral . . .	—	ib.

This is a very singular ornament, and consists of two rows of stones, the semicircular ends of which project at right angles from the wall, but it produces a very good effect.

	PAGE	PLATE
Bredgar, Kent	—	ib.

This is the nail-head cut alternately on the upper and lower face of a three-sided moulding, and is another example of what might be easily converted into a tooth ornament, and the same may be said of

	PAGE	PLATE
MOULDINGS AND ORNAMENTS. Iffley and North Hinksey. The indented is much used in transition work, and sometimes in Early English.		
Indented. 1. Iffley, Oxfordshire. 2. S. Nicholas, Norwich	—	116
Ditto, North Hinksey, Berks	—	ib.
Beak-head. S. Ebbe's, Oxford	—	117
Cat's-head. Tickencote, Rutland . . .	—	ib.
Ditto, West door, Lincoln cathedral . . .	—	ib.
Ditto, Charney, Berks	—	ib.
See also CAPITAL, Nun Monkton, p. 110. These are all varieties of a mode of ornament much used in the richest period of Norman for ornamenting doorways, windows, and arches. The one from Lincoln is from the rich door of Bishop Alexander, and shews the double as well as the single head. Very fine examples of both occur also at Iffley.		
Bird's head. S. Cross, Hants	—	ib.
This occurs on a window, and is a very beautiful variation of the mode of filling up a zigzag.		
Scolloped. Hadiscoe, Norfolk. Castor, Northamptonshire	—	ib.
The scollop is an ornament frequently used either by itself or in combination with others.		
Interrupted arched. S. Alban's abbey church . .	—	ib.
Label corbel-table. S. Julian's, Norwich . .	—	ib.
Nebule corbel-table. S. Peter at Gowt's, Lincoln .	—	ib.
Binham Priory, Norfolk	—	ib.
These are two varieties of the waved line or nebule which is not unfrequently used as a corbel-table.		
Pellet. Door, Iffley, Oxfordshire . . .	—	118
The doors and arches of this fine church present a great variety of details, two of which are here given; viz., the pellet, which is an ornament very frequently in use, and the rose, which is more unusual.		
Studded. Hales, Norfolk	—	ib.
Fir-cone or Fir-apple. Croyland abbey, Lincolnshire .	—	ib.
This is a variety of the pellet, but being cross-hatched gives it the appearance of a fir-cone.		
Rose. Door, Iffley, Oxon	—	ib.
Ditto, Nun Monkton, Yorkshire . . .	—	ib.
Is another variety, and occurs here in transition almost Early English work. A form very similar is found in the work of Bishop Alexander		

MOULDINGS AND ORNAMENTS.

	PAGE	PLATE
at Lincoln, Plate 114, in the Early English work in the choir at Lincoln as a hoodmould termination, and again at S. Mary's, Beverley, Plate 127. It seems therefore to have been a favourite form, though it is impossible to say what it is intended to represent.		
1. *Diamond fretté.* Lincoln cathedral, c. 1140	—	118
The two examples here given occur in the work of Bishop Alexander so often mentioned.		
Chain. S. William's chapel, York	—	ib.
The chain moulding is not common, and the chapel from which this was taken is now entirely destroyed.		
Double cone. Stoneleigh, Warwickshire	—	ib.
This is not of common occurrence; an example differently arranged is shewn in Plate 113.		
Triangular fretté or *dovetail.* Ely cathedral	—	ib.
2. *Embattled.* Lincoln cathedral	—	ib.
Trellis and *Medallion.* Malmsbury abbey	—	119
These two ornaments are much used in rich Norman work, the first for enriching the shafts, and the latter for the arches of doors, &c., where the medallions are generally filled with the signs of the zodiac and other subjects.		
Open heart and *Antique.* Jew's House, Lincoln	—	ib.
These, the second of which is an evident imitation of Grecian ornament, are taken from the fine twelfth-century house known as the Jew's House in Lincoln, and which appears to be of about the same date as the next example.		
3. West door, Lincoln cathedral, c. 1145	—	ib.
The work of Bishop Alexander. The specimen here given is an abacus of one of the shafts.		
Overlapping. S. Margaret's, York	—	ib.
This is an uncommon and very curious example, the ornament appearing to lie over the mouldings which are seen through the openings.		
Patricksbourne, Kent	—	ib.
These appear to belong to the same class as Malmsbury.		
4. West door, Lincoln, c. 1145	—	ib.
This is another example from the work of Alexander so often mentioned. It, as well as the three following examples, have a strong resemblance to the tooth ornament, but the differences are pointed out in Plate 112.		

	PAGE	PLAT
MOULDINGS AND ORNAMENTS.		
Patricksbourne, Kent	—	119
Canterbury cathedral, c. 1180	—	ib.

From the so-called baptistery at Canterbury. (See Willis's Canterbury cathedral, p. 82.)

NORMAN and TRANSITION . . . .   —   120

The whole of the examples in this Plate are transitional.

Nun Monkton, Yorkshire, c. 1180 . . .   —   ib.

This is taken from a small but highly interesting and curious church, which is for the most part Early English, but has many portions which have more or less of Norman or Transition character about them, and of this class is the west doorway from which this section is taken. It is an excellent specimen of transition, though it has more of Norman than Early English character. The profile retains the general square form of the Norman, but the angle moulding is keeled, and the hollows on each side are enlarged. The ornament is an enriched zigzag which overlies the keeled moulding, allowing it only to be seen through the intervals. (See Arch. Journal, vol. iv. p. 131.)

Canterbury cathedral, c. 1178 . . . .   —   ib.

This is a rib-moulding from the work of William of Sens, and has much of transition character about it, for though in general appearance it is Norman, the deep hollows of the moulding and the almost entire loss of the original squareness of the whole mass, approximate it to Early English.

Ratcliffe, Bucks, c. 1180 . . . .   —   ib.

In this again the zigzags form lozenges, but they are not pierced as in the last example. An obtuse tooth ornament is used in the drip-stone.

Cuddesden, Oxfordshire, c. 1180 . . .   —   ib.

The ornament here is produced by the meeting of two zigzags on the angle, and by cutting away the stone of the alternate spaces they are left detached, and the large round moulding shewn underneath. A small tooth ornament is also used.

Hargrave, Northamptonshire, c. 1200 . . .   —   ib.

In this almost all Norman features have disappeared except the disjointed chevrons which lie over the hollow mouldings. The tooth is used, and the mouldings are more rounded than in the preceding examples.

Glastonbury abbey, c. 1180 . . . .   —   ib.

This is a portion of one of the doorways, and is of transition charac-

Mouldings from the choir of the Temple Church, London.

	PAGE	PLATE
MOULDINGS AND ORNAMENTS.		
It consists of a series of squares enclosing circles and quatrefoils, which are very deeply cut, so that the centres stand in very bold relief.		
Peterborough cathedral, c. 1240	—	124
Winchester cathedral, c. 1260 .	—	ib.
Transition. Dorchester, Oxfordshire, c. 1280 n.	—	122
Window, north aisle, Dorchester, Oxfordshire, c. 1280 .	—	ib.
Both these sections, particularly the first, belong to the transition or geometrical period.		
Bishop Bridport's tomb, Salisbury cathedral, A.D. 1246.	—	124
Warmington, Northamptonshire, c. 1250	—	ib.
Old organ-screen, Salisbury cathedral, A.D. 1258 (two examples) .	—	ib.
Ely, Peterborough, Winchester, Warmington, and Salisbury shew different applications of the characteristic trefoil, and other varieties of foliage.		
DECORATED. Ely cathedral, c. 1330	—	125
Howden, Yorkshire	—	ib.
Selby, Yorkshire	—	ib.
Dorchester, Oxfordshire, c. 1320	—	ib.
Headington, Oxfordshire, c. 1300	—	ib.
By comparing this plate with that of the Early English, it will be seen that there is a great difference of character. The hollows are not so deep, and the rounds are scarcely undercut, and the fillets are more common. The one from Headington exhibits a moulding which seems to be peculiar to this style. This is what may be called a *sunk chamfer*, and consists of a chamfer with a small square cut on its upper and lower edge, and thus by the light and shade produced adding greater distinctness to the outline.		
East window, Great Haseley, Oxfordshire, c. 1300	—	126
Door, N. aisle, Great Haseley, c. 1350 .	—	ib.
Thorpe Malsor, Northamptonshire	—	ib.
Door, Kiddington, Oxfordshire, c. 1350 .	—	ib.
Window, Great Haseley, Oxfordshire, c. 1350 .	—	ib.
Window, Little Wenham hall, Suffolk, c. 1300	—	ib.
The whole of these examples exhibit different varieties of the scroll moulding in their hood-moulds, and the first one from Haseley shews also the inner arch of the window, or as it is sometimes called, rear arch, or escoinson arch.		

MOULDINGS AND ORNAMENTS.

The following examples from S. Stephen's chapel are introduced here, as being particularly good, and somewhat different from any given in the Plates.

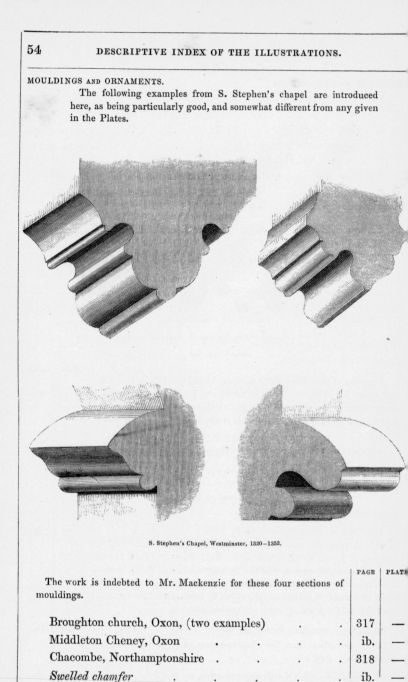

S. Stephen's Chapel, Westminster, 1320—1352.

	PAGE	PLATE
The work is indebted to Mr. Mackenzie for these four sections of mouldings.		
Broughton church, Oxon, (two examples) . .	317	—
Middleton Cheney, Oxon	ib.	—
Chacombe, Northamptonshire . . .	318	—
Swelled chamfer	ib.	—

OULDINGS AND ORNAMENTS.
York cathedral.

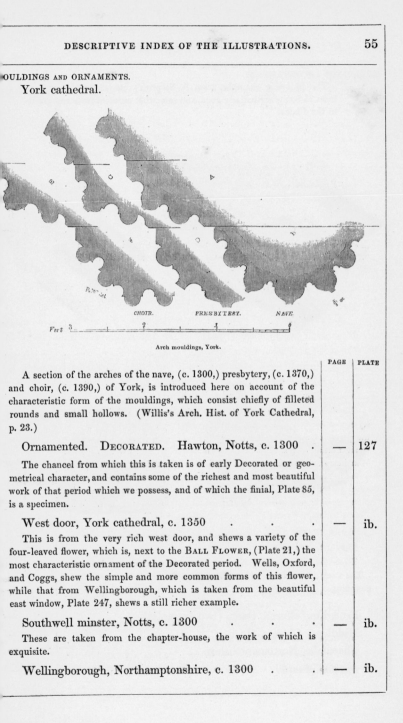

CHOIR. PRESBYTERY. NAVE.

Feet 3 2 1 0

Arch mouldings, York.

	PAGE	PLATE

A section of the arches of the nave, (c. 1300,) presbytery, (c. 1370,) and choir, (c. 1390,) of York, is introduced here on account of the characteristic form of the mouldings, which consist chiefly of filleted rounds and small hollows. (Willis's Arch. Hist. of York Cathedral, p. 23.)

Ornamented. DECORATED. Hawton, Notts, c. 1300 . — 127

The chancel from which this is taken is of early Decorated or geo-metrical character, and contains some of the richest and most beautiful work of that period which we possess, and of which the finial, Plate 85, is a specimen.

West door, York cathedral, c. 1350 . . . — ib.

This is from the very rich west door, and shews a variety of the four-leaved flower, which is, next to the BALL FLOWER, (Plate 21,) the most characteristic ornament of the Decorated period. Wells, Oxford, and Coggs, shew the simple and more common forms of this flower, while that from Wellingborough, which is taken from the beautiful east window, Plate 247, shews a still richer example.

Southwell minster, Notts, c. 1300 . . . — ib.

These are taken from the chapter-house, the work of which is exquisite.

Wellingborough, Northamptonshire, c. 1300 . . — ib.

MOULDINGS AND ORNAMENTS.

	PAGE	PLATE
S. Mary's, Beverley, c. 1300	—	127

This has been referred to before under Plate 114.

Door, Adderbury, Oxon, c. 1330	—	ib.

Is a very fine church, the south doorway, from which this is taken, containing a great variety of rich detail.

Southwell minster, Notts, c. 1300	—	ib.
Lady Chapel, Wells cathedral, c. 1330	—	ib.
North window, Coggs, Oxon, c. 1350	—	ib.
Latin chapel, Oxford cathedral, c. 1350	—	ib.
Dorchester church, Oxfordshire	318	—

This is the moulding of the doorway on page 180, vol. i. The centre member is remarkable, being grooved and ornamented with the four-leaved flower.

Steventon church, Berkshire	ib.	—

PERPENDICULAR. Door of refectory, cloisters, Norwich,

A.D. 1415	—	128
Pier-arch, presbytery, Norwich, A.D. 1480	—	ib.
West door, Emneth, Norfolk	—	ib.
Nave, Winchester cathedral	—	ib.
Hen. VIIth's chapel, Westminster abbey	—	ib.
West door, Iselham, Cambridgeshire	—	ib.

This is a plate of the most characteristic forms of mouldings of this style, and differences will be best understood by comparing them with the plates of the preceding styles. The cloister, Norwich, shews the small rounds and shallow hollows so frequently met with. Emneth, Winchester, Westminster, and Iselham shew a form which is very much used, the double ogee or brace-moulding, which consists of two ogees cut in opposite directions. Westminster and Iselham shew also the deep wide hollow so often met with in doors and windows. Winchester shews the most common form of hoodmould.

Window, east end of north aisle, Great Haseley, Oxford-

shire, c. 1430	—	129

This shews more clearly the wide hollow in windows and doorways, and is altogether a very characteristic example.

Clerestory window, Fotheringhay, Northamptonshire,

A.D. 1440	—	ib.
West door, Fotheringhay, A.D. 1440 (two examples)	—	ib.
West window, Fotheringhay, A.D. 1440	—	ib.

All the details from this church are valuable from the date being so well known, because the contract for the building of it is still extant. The

	PAGE	PLATE

MOULDINGS OF BASEMENTS.

Southwell minster, Nottinghamshire, c. 1220 .   .   —   132

The first is from the choir of Lincoln, and is remarkable for the great boldness of its mouldings by which that portion of the building is characterized. Southwell, though not so bold, is a very good example.

DECORATED. Leadenham, Lincolnshire, c. 1330   .   —   ib.

Grantham, Lincolnshire, c. 1330   .   .   .   —   ib.

These are both marked by the distinctive mouldings of the style, but the one from Leadenham is unusually rich.

PERPENDICULAR. New College, Oxford, A.D. 1386.
S. Mary's, Oxford, A.D. 1488 .   .   .   .   —   ib.

MOULDINGS OF STRINGS. NORMAN. Peterborough cathedral, c. 1140 .   .   .   .   .   —   133

Ely cathedral, c. 1140 .   .   .   .   .   —   ib.

These are both from large fine buildings, and are highly ornamented, but though *strings* are frequently cut in various ways, they are more commonly plain and of the form of the abacus, that is square with the lower side chamfered, or with both sides chamfered.

EARLY ENGLISH. Choir, Lincoln, c. 1200   .   .   —   ib.

S. Sepulchre's, Northampton, c. 1220 .   .   —   ib.

The first is from the choir at Lincoln, Plate 38, where it is very much used. The second, the sharp-keeled moulding, is a very common form, and much used in country churches.

Romsey, Hampshire, c. 1250 .   .   .   .   —   ib.

Salisbury cathedral, c. 1240 .   .   .   .   —   ib.

DECORATED. Merton college chapel, Oxford, A.D. 1277   —   ib.

Sedgebarrow, Worcestershire, c. 1360 .   .   .   —   ib.

Warmington, Warwickshire, c. 1350 .   .   .   —   ib.

Finedon, Northamptonshire, c. 1340 .   .   .   —   ib.

Merton and Finedon exhibit two forms of the roll moulding. They are both much used, particularly the latter. Warmington is unusually deep and bold.

PERPENDICULAR. Magdalene college, Oxford, A.D. 1480 .   .   .   .   .   .   —   ib

Wilby, Northamptonshire, c. 1450 .   .   .   —   ib

These are two of very common occurrence. The one from Magdalene does not differ materially from that at Sedgebarrow, except that the latter has greater boldness of curve in the upper moulding, and a chamfer instead of a small round moulding below.

	PAGE	PLATE
MOULDINGS OF RIBS. NORMAN. Gloucester crypt, A.D. 1100 (two examples)	—	134
The first example exhibits a massive square rib without mouldings, the next is little more than circular.		
TRANSITION. Oxford cathedral, c. 1180, and Glastonbury abbey, c. 1190	—	ib.
Is a form of very frequent occurrence.		
EARLY ENGLISH. Salisbury cathedral, A.D. 1250 .	—	ib.
S. Saviour's, Southwark, c. 1250 (two examples) .	—	ib.
Temple church, London, A.D. 1240 . . .	—	ib.
Four different forms are here given, but those from Salisbury and S. Saviour's are the most usual.		
DECORATED. Gloucester cathedral, c. 1300, and c. 1318. (Two examples.)	—	ib.
The second is the most general form, but it is here decorated with the ball-flower, which gives it greater richness. (See Plate 221.)		
PERPENDICULAR. New College, Oxford, A.D. 1386 .	—	ib.
Divinity School, Oxford, c. 1450 . . .	—	ib.
These are both good and common forms. Another, perhaps more usual one, is the New College one with a plain round substituted for the filleted moulding.		
FLAMBOYANT	209	—
MOULDING TERMINATIONS. Warmington, Northamptonshire	—	135
Westminster abbey	—	ib.
Salisbury cathedral	—	ib.
Rothwell, Northamptonshire	—	ib.
Canterbury cathedral	—	ib.
Finedon, Northamptonshire	—	ib.
Bayham abbey, Sussex	—	ib.
Pitsford, Northamptonshire	—	ib.
Finedon, Northamptonshire	—	ib.
This Plate exhibits the various modes used in the Early English and Decorated styles of ornamenting the junction of a chamfer and a square. The chamfer, sometimes plain and sometimes hollow, is much used on the inner splays of windows and in door jambs, and indeed in every situation where it was necessary for the admission of light or for the		

	PAGE	PLAT.

MOULDING TERMINATIONS.
sake of effect to take off the square angle. The junction of these has been laid hold of as an opportunity of adding ornament to plain surfaces, and the ingenuity and beauty with which this has been executed is surprising. One of the most elegant is that from Warmington, which is filled up with Early English foliage. The one from Finedon shews the most usual mode of finishing the upper and lower terminations of the chamfer of a window splay, that at Rothwell is on a large scale in the window in the tower, and the one from Salisbury is on a buttress.

NORMAN STYLE.

THE PERPENDICULAR STYLE.

PERPEYN WALL. Lincoln cathedral, c. 1200 . . 351 —

This is one of the dwarf walls or solid screens which divide the
chapels on the east side of the transept.

PEW. DECORATED. Dol, Brittany, c. 1300 . . 353 —

A very curious and early example, with early Decorated tracery.

PERPENDICULAR. Irchester, Northamptonshire, c. 1450. — 143
Finedon, Northamptonshire, c. 1450 . . — ib.

These two are very fine examples of wooden panelling. At Finedon,
nearly the whole church still has its original open seats of this character.

Nettlecombe, Somersetshire, c. 1500 . . . — ib.

A late but very good and uncommon specimen, ornamented with
foliage; this engraving is repeated by accident in the text, p. 352.

Kidlington, Oxfordshire, c. 1450 . . . — ib.

A good example of an end pew with the return and diagonal buttresses, ornamented with the monograms of the name of Christ.

Milverton, Somersetshire, c. 1540 . . . — 144

The arms on this pew are those of Henry VIII.; on another corresponding exactly with this is the date 1540 as part of the ornament.

Braunton, Devonshire, c. 1500 . . . — ib

This is one of a set of fine old pews with which this church is fitted,
on several of them are the different instruments of the crucifixion; on
this one the ladder and the hammer are represented. These implements
are often called the emblems of the crucifixion, and are most exten-

PAGE   PLAT

PILLAR. NORMAN. S. Peter's, Northampton, c. 1140   356   —
     Geddington, Northamptonshire, c. 1150   .   .   —   147
     Islip, Oxfordshire, c. 1180   .   .   .   .   —   ib
     Appleton, Berkshire, c. 1180   .   .   .   .   —   ib

Notwithstanding the dwarfish and heavy character of the two last examples, they belong to the period of transition, as shewn by the mouldings of the bases, and they have pointed arches.

     Four plans   .   .   .   .   356 and   357   —

EARLY ENGLISH. Lincoln cathedral, choir, c. 1200   .   —   ib

The crockets between the main pillar and the detached shafts are a very unusual feature, they are shewn also in the section of the pillar, Plate 150.

     Salisbury cathedral, choir, c. 1250, or rather perhaps
       1225, the year that the eastern part was conse-
       crated   .   .   .   .   .   .   —   ib

This example shews the detached shafts.

     Salisbury cathedral, nave, c. 1250   .   .   .   —   ib

In this the shafts are attached.

     Welford, Northamptonshire, c. 1250   .   .   .   ib.   —

A good example of the rather clumsy character which we frequently find in country churches, even in this elegant style.

     The Minstrel's Pillar, S. Mary's, Beverley   .   .   ib.

This engraving is presented to the work by the liberality of J. H. Markland, Esq., of Bath, it is taken from his valuable little work, the "Remarks on English Churches, and on the expediency of Sepulchral Memorials subservient to pious and Christian uses," in the hope that this beautiful example of the good taste of the minstrels of those days, may induce others to go and do likewise. How much better it would be for all parties, if the executors of a person deceased, would enquire if the church in which it is proposed to erect a monument to his memory could not be improved by a new window, a new porch, or a new pillar, which might serve for the monument, instead of the hideous pagan deformities, or the mere patches of black and white marble with which our churches are commonly disfigured.

DECORATED. Orton-on-the-hill, Leicestershire, c. 1350 .   —   148
     Wymington, Bedfordshire, c. 1380   .   .   .   —   ib
     S. Michael's, Oxford, c. 1380   .   .   .   .   —   ib

Wymington is an uncommon and curious example from having channels cut in the face of the pillar, and not carried through to the

	PAGE	PLATE
INNACLE.		
DECORATED. S. Mary's, Oxford, c. 1300 .	—	ib.

This celebrated and beautiful cluster of pinnacles is now being re-built (June 1850), the lower part with the canopies very faithfully restored, the upper part from the set-off had been previously rebuilt in the time of Charles I., and it is impossible to say how far the original design had been then exactly copied, but they are here represented as they are believed to have been originally built, preserving the proportions and the outlines exactly as they were handed down to us from the time of Charles I., and restoring the details only. In the new pinnacles a second set of canopies is introduced at the set-off, and the upper part of the pinnacle is carried up six feet higher than it was before.

For other details of this beautiful tower and spire see the cornice, Plate 63; a mullion, Plate 136; the parapet, Plate 139; one of the spire lights, Plate 258. The exact date is not known but is believed to be from 1280 to 1300.

	PAGE	PLATE
PERPENDICULAR. John of Gaunt's palace, Lincoln	361	—
S. Stephen's, Bristol	359	—

The projecting wing of this pinnacle is now destroyed, but at Thornbury (Plate 140) they still remain: this appears to have been a fashion in late examples of the rich Perpendicular churches in the west of England.

This is a curious example of a kind of turret, or pinnacle, not uncommon in rich towers in the west of England, having a flying or hanging buttress at the outer angle.

For other pinnacles see also PORCH, Plate 165, and p. 209; PARAPET, Plate 140; TURRET, p. 50; MONUMENT, p. 311.

	PAGE	PLATE
PISCINA. NORMAN. Crowmarsh Giffard, Oxfordshire, c. 1120	—	155
Kirkstall abbey, Yorkshire, c. 1160 . . .	—	ib.
Towersay, Buckinghamshire, c. 1150 . . .	—	ib.
Ryarsh, Kent, c. 1150	—	ib.
EARLY ENGLISH. Higham Ferrers, Northamptonshire, c. 1250	—	156
Rushden, Northamptonshire, c. 1250 . . .	—	ib.
Cowling, Suffolk, c. 1260	—	ib.

This example is remarkable for the richness of the mouldings.

	PAGE	PLATE
Warmington, Northamptonshire . . .	361	—
DECORATED. Fyfield, Berkshire, c. 1350 . .	—	ib.
Long Wittenham, Berkshire, 1300 . . .	—	ib.

A curious example of a piscina and monument combined, having a diminutive effigy across the basin.

	PAGE	PLATE

A fair specimen of the panelled oak pulpits of the Perpendicular style, which are common in some districts, especially in Somersetshire and the west of England, and in Norfolk. The ceiling of the original small canopy with its fan-tracery is shewn under the sounding-board of the time of James I. A fine example of the canopy over a pulpit entire from Eddlesborough, Bucks, is given on p. 452.

The two last are of stone, the two previous of wood; that at Frampton has some curious sculptures upon it, one figure is evidently that of a priest or a saint holding up the monstrance; that at Coventry was restored by Mr. Rickman.

This, which is now built into the wall of the north transept, represents our Saviour and the twelve Apostles under tabernacles. The figures from their emblems appear to be, 1. S. Peter; 2. S. Philip; 3. S. James the Greater; 4. S. James the Less; 5. S. Andrew; 6. S. Matthew; 7. S. Bartholomew; 8. S. Matthias (?); 9. S. Jude; 10. S. Simon (?); 11. S. Thomas; 12. S. John. The length of the sculpture is 6 ft. 10 in., and breadth 2 ft. 1 in.

This, which is in its proper place under the east window, is surrounded with a modern wooden frame. It represents the Last Supper. There appear at first to be only ten Apostles shewn, but on examining it, it will be found that the subject is taken from the gospel of S. John where the Evangelist is said to be "lying on Jesus' breast," and this it will be seen has been *literally* rendered. The time chosen is after the departure of Judas, and this accounts for there being only eleven. The length is 8 ft. 6½ in., and height 2 ft. 1 in.

Section of roof, S. Mary's, Beverley.

This subject is strictly more of an open gallery front than a screen; over the east end of the chancel of this church is a vault supporting an upper floor, formerly used as a chapel, which is open to the church, except that there is a low parapet in front, on which stands the range of wooden arches here represented.

This elegant screen is probably Early English work, the details corresponding with the stone-work of the chancel in which it is placed.

Base of Shafts.   Capital of Shafts.   Arch.

SCREEN.

	PAGE	PLATE
EARLY DECORATED. Northfleet, Kent, c. 1300 . . .	—	182

A valuable specimen both of screen-work and iron-work of the early Decorated period, the mouldings are very characteristic and are here given.

Base of Shafts.   Capital of Shafts.   Cornice and Arch.

	PAGE	PLATE
Stone screen, choir, Canterbury cathedral, A.D. 1304 .	—	ib.

For an interesting history and description of this, see Professor Willis's Canterbury Cathedral, p. 97.

DECORATED. Shotswell, Oxfordshire, c. 1350 . .	—	183

This church contains a good deal of original wood-work.

Geddington, Northamptonshire, c. 1360 . .	—	ib.
Cropredy, Northamptonshire, c. 1350 . . .	—	ib.
Sparsholt, Berks	416	—
PERPENDICULAR. Fyfield, Berks, c. 1480 . .	—	184

This is a valuable example of the arrangement of a chantry chapel.

S. Mary's, Leicester, c. 1450	—	ib.
OPEN TRACERY and PANEL TRACERY. Rushden, North-amptonshire, c. 1450, (four examples) . .	—	185

Rushden is a particularly fine church, and contains a good deal of rich screen-work. The examples here given are from a screen in the north aisle, now much mutilated. The two upper ones are from the open part of the screen, and the two lower from that which is laid on the boards of the panels.

S. Giles's, Northampton, c. 1450 . . .	—	ib.

This is part of the chancel-screen in the north aisle.

	PAGE	PLATE

TILES.

the Lady-chapel and the Latin chapel, and are of various dates. Some of the patterns occupy only a single tile, in others it takes four, and in the lower one on Plate 201 sixteen tiles would be required to make the pattern complete.

Library of Merton college, Oxford, A.D. 1377 · — 201

These pave the path in the centre of the library, which has a boarded floor. The tiles are in general in a much worn state, so that in some instances they are difficult to make out. They seem all of one date except the first, which is of earlier character. Those which have letters are very curious, but it is difficult to understand the meaning of them. It is very possible that others which would have helped to make out words with these, have been lost.

Woodperry, Oxfordshire · · · 469 203

These, which are all of Early English character, were found in digging on the site of the destroyed church of Woodperry, and along with them some coffin-slabs in their original situation. For an interesting account of them, see a paper by the Rev. J. Wilson, Archæol. Journal, vol. iii. p. 116.

Old singing school, Worcester cathedral · · — 204

TILE PAVING. Old singing school, Worcester cathedral — 205

This Plate exhibits in the upper example a very valuable piece of tile paving, shewing the complete arrangement of an entire room, and Plate 204 shews some of the patterns on a larger scale. The date seems to be early in the fourteenth century, and the foliage, particularly of the sixteen tile pattern on Plate 204, is like all the ornaments of that period, bold, free, and elegant. The introduction of black tiles among the coloured ones is a great relief to the eye. The two lower examples on Plate 205 are from other parts near the former one.

Ditto. Plate 206. 1. Great Bedwin, Wilts · · — 20

The black lines shew the division of the tiles. The centre of the circle is made up of four tiles, the circle itself of twelve, and the spandrels of two tiles each, making in the whole twenty-four. On two sides of it are plain yellow border tiles, and outside these, ornamented border tiles.

2. All Saints, Leicester · · · · — i

3. S. Alban's abbey, Herts · · · · — i

4. Brookham · · · · · · — i

5. Beaulieu abbey, Wilts · · · · — i

These four are border tiles.

6. Helpstone, Northamptonshire · · · — i

This is from the same church as Plate 209.

TILE PAVING.

	PAGE	PLATE
7. Wells cathedral	—	20 6

This is a purely architectural and very uncommon design.

Rochester cathedral (five examples) . . .	—	207
Winchester cathedral	—	ib.
Haccombe, Devonshire	—	208

Is a small but very interesting church. For an account of the tiles, see Archæol. Journal, vol. iii. p. 151.

Helpstone, Northamptonshire	—	209

This is the paving of the altar platform, the lozenge border being the edge of the step.

Pan tiles	463	—
Inlaid tiles, Canterbury cathedral . . .	465	—
Flanders tiles, Westleigh, Devonshire . . .	472	—

It is rather difficult to affix dates to these tiles, but the following arrangement is believed to be nearly accurate.

Of the twelfth century. Canterbury . .	465	—

Of the early part of the thirteenth century.
Plate 198, Nos. 6, 15, 16, 18, 19, 20, 27.
Plate 199, No. 8.
Helpstone, Plate 206, No. 6; and Plate 209.
Rochester, Plate 207.
Winchester, Plate 207.
Brookham, Plate 206, No. 4.

Late in the thirteenth century.
Plate 198, Nos. 1—10.
Oxford cathedral, Plate 200, Nos. 1—7, 9—11;
    Plate 201, Nos. 1, 2, 5—7, 15, 17, 20, 21.
Leicester, Plate 206, No. 2; Beaulieu, Plate 206, No. 5.
Woodperry, Plate 203.
Worcester, Plate 204 and 205.

Of the fourteenth century.
Plate 198, Nos. 11—14, 17, 21, 22, 24, 26.
Plate 199, Nos. 1, 2, 11.
Oxford cathedral, Plate 200, Nos. 8, 12, 13;
    Plate 201, Nos. 4, 8, 9, 12—14, 16, 18, 19.
Oxford, Merton Library, Plate 202.
Great Bedwin, Pl. 206, No. 1; S. Alban's, Pl. 206, No. 3.
Wells, Plate 206, No. 7.
Haccombe, Plate 208, Nos. 3, 10, 11.

TILE PAVING.   PAGE   PLA
    OF THE FIFTEENTH CENTURY.
        Plate 198. Nos. 23, 25, 28.
        Plate 199. Nos. 3—7, 9, 10.
        Oxford cathedral, Plate 201, Nos. 3, 10, 11.
    The following armorial bearings occur in the tiles here given.
        Plate 198. No. 9. is the griffin of the Despenser family ;
            28. the arms of Sebrok, abbot of Gloucester in 1450.
        Plate 199. No. 3. the arms of the family of Clare;
            No. 4. England and France, quarterly in the time of
            Henry VI.; 5. and 7. England and the Confessor in
            the same reign, " Anno 1453."
        Plate 204. Worcester. No. 3. Richard Plantagenet,
            earl of Cornwall and king of the Romans.
        Plate 205. Border, first row, Digby, second, Clare. No.
            5. Warren; 6. Beauchamp; 7. England; 10. Ver-
            dun, Willoughby or Hodelston.
        Plate 201. Oxford cathedral. No. 3. See of Exeter ;
            19. England.
        Plate 208. Haccombe. No. 6. England: 7. Ercedechne,
            or Archdeacon ; 9. Haccombe.

TOOTH ORNAMENT   475   —
    Nun Monkton, Yorkshire   .   .   . 476   —
    Canterbury cathedral. (See also Plate 123) .   . ib.   —
TORUS   .   .   .   . ib.   —
TOWER. Supposed SAXON. Sompting, Sussex   .   . —   21

    This is a very singular and valuable example of Saxon. Each side
terminates in a gable evidently original, and these support a diagonal
roof. This kind of termination has a great resemblance to some of
the German churches, but is, as far as is known, unique in England,
though it was probably the mode in which many Saxon towers ter-
minated originally.

    Earl's Barton, Northamptonshire   .   .   . 407   —
    Round tower, Devenish Island, Lough Erne, Ireland . 412   —
    Dunham Magna, Norfolk   478   —
    S. Peter at Gowt's, Lincoln, c. 1070   .   .   . —   ib

    This in a chronological view is very valuable, as forming a con-
necting link between the Saxon and early Norman. There seems
good evidence that it was built immediately after the Norman conquest, but by the Saxon inhabitants of the city, and it displays most
of the peculiarities of the Saxon style, but of better workmanship than

	PAGE	PLATE
TOWER.		
usual, and with some mixture of early Norman features. The neighbouring tower of S. Mary le Wigford is another example of the same date. The history of these two towers is well made out in the " Introduction to Gothic Architecture," Oxford, 1849, p. 33.		
S. Julian's, Norwich	—	210
One of the round flint towers so common in Norfolk, where they appear to be almost of all dates. This of S. Julian is apparently Norman, with later windows inserted.		
Warneford, Hampshire, c. 1170	—	ib.
An inscription over the door of this church records its rebuilding by Adam de Port, who held the manor during the reigns of Henry II., Richard I., and John. See Arch. Journal, vol. ii. p. 191.		
Little Saxham church, Suffolk	481	—
EARLY ENGLISH. Middleton Stoney, Oxon, c. 1220	—	211
This shews the very characteristic arcade through which the windows are pierced, in the upper story. The buttresses both in this and the next example are rather peculiar.		
Bishop Cannings, Wiltshire, c. 1220	—	ib.
A rich and beautiful example, exhibiting two corbel-tables and triple belfry windows, the composition of the tower and transept is very good.		
Brookthorpe, Northamptonshire, c. 1250	—	ib.
This and the following are examples of gabled or pack-saddle roofs.		
Ickford, Bucks	482	—
Versainville, c. 1250	—	ib.
Mortain, Normandy	483	—
DECORATED. Ravensthorpe, Northamptonshire, c. 1300	—	212
Coggs, Oxfordshire, c. 1350	—	ib.
A curious tower, belonging to an interesting little church.		
Church Brampton, Northamptonshire, c. 1340	—	ib.
An example of diagonal buttresses on a tower.		
TRANSITION. Little Harrowden, Northamptonshire, c. 1370	—	ib.
This is almost Perpendicular, but the tracery of the window is Decorated.		
PERPENDICULAR. Welford, Northamptonshire	—	213
The buttresses are rather peculiar, but are found on several churches in the county, they are neither diagonal nor parallel, but are *angle-clasping*, as we sometimes find in earlier examples.		
Cromer, Norfolk	—	ib.
This tower is of squared flint with the quoins and mouldings of		

This is a remarkable little building, the roof being of stone and supported on stone ribs in the manner of a timber roof. A view of the interior is given in Rickman's Architecture, fifth edition, p. 179.

This building is of squared flint, and exhibits in its parapet and basement the flat panelling of flint and stone so frequent in Norfolk.

This is an early example. The arch of the window is turned with Roman tiles, but it differs from most Saxon windows in not having an external splay.

A small church with a tower of Saxon character; the windows are extremely small and rude, so as scarcely to be called windows. The opening for light is pierced through a single stone, and they have a wide splay both internally and externally.

S. Peter at Gowt's, Lincoln.

The names of these two churches are Saxon, and they appear to be of a date immediately after the Conquest; Le Wigford signifies at the wick ford; see pl. 210: At Gowt's signifies at the sluices, the land having then been first drained from the marsh. Immediately over this window is a figure of S. Peter, which is here given.

Deerhurst, Gloucestershire, A.D. 1056 . . | — | 22

Is an example of the triangular-headed window so frequent in this style, but this is a much richer specimen than is generally found.

inner one has an octofoil in the head and is supported on slender shafts, some single and some clustered. The effect of the two from the reflected light between is frequently highly beautiful.

It has been customary to consider Salisbury cathedral as belonging to the middle of the thirteenth century, about 1240 or 1250, and a great part of the building is undoubtedly of that date, but the eastern part is earlier, though it is doubtful how far this early part of the work extends. The history tells us that the foundations were laid in 1220.

Deanery, Norwich, c. 1250   .   .   .   .   — 23

In this the spandrels are pierced and the openings are well moulded, forming an example of early tracery. The fillet springs from the external wall.

Charlton on Otmoor, Oxon, 1250   .   .   .   — il

This is similar to the last example, but it is not moulded, and the spandrels are sunk instead of being pierced.

GROUPED LANCETS. Wimborne minster, Dorset, c. 1220 .   — 23

In this, though the lancets with the openings above are separate on the outside, they are in the interior combined into one general design.

Headington, Oxfordshire, c. 1240   .   .   .   — il
Warmington, Northamptonshire, c. 1240   .   .   — il
Ditto, c. 1250 .   .   .   .   .   — il

These are examples of three lancets brought together and combined under one dripstone.

Uffington, Berkshire, c 1220   .   .   .   .   — 23

A very singular example, in which the head of the window is made to take the form of the gable in which it is placed, at the back of a small recess for an altar. There are several of these recesses on the east side of both the transepts. The church is altogether a very remarkable one, and worthy of more attention than it has received.

Amesbury, Wiltshire, c. 1250   420   -

A good example of an unglazed window in a gable, the tracery is a kind of mixture of plate tracery and bar tracery.

Romsey abbey, Hampshire, c. 1250   .   .   .   — 2
S. John's church, Winchester, c. 1250   .   .   — 2
S. Mary le Wigford, Lincoln, c. 1220, with cusps   .   — 2(

This is from the east end of this very interesting church, where it combines with the two lancets below, and forms one of the first steps towards plate tracery.

The front is here given as a good example of a plain Early English east end, shewing the arrangement of the windows.

WINDOWS—EARLY ENGLISH.

	PAGE	PLATE

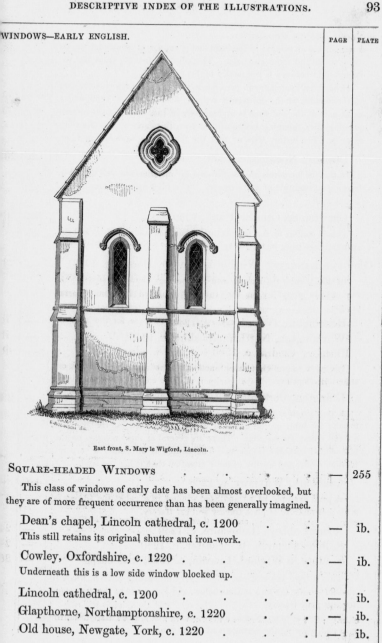

East front, S. Mary le Wigford, Lincoln.

SQUARE-HEADED WINDOWS . . . . — 255

    This class of windows of early date has been almost overlooked, but they are of more frequent occurrence than has been generally imagined.

    Dean's chapel, Lincoln cathedral, c. 1200 . . — ib.
This still retains its original shutter and iron-work.

    Cowley, Oxfordshire, c. 1220 . . . — ib.
Underneath this is a low side window blocked up.

    Lincoln cathedral, c. 1200 . . . — ib.

    Glapthorne, Northamptonshire, c. 1220 . . — ib.

    Old house, Newgate, York, c. 1220 . . . — ib.

These are examples of different proportions of the pointed oval, or *vesica piscis* as it is often called.

A good specimen of plate tracery. The rest on the plate are Decorated.

This is of much the same design as Barfreston, but is decidedly Early English. It is an excellent illustration of plate tracery, and shews clearly the piercing through the solid plate of stone for the sake of light before the idea had occurred of forming it into tracery.

This is in the north transept, and is part of the original work of Bishop Hugh. It is also a specimen of plate tracery, and is perhaps the richest and most beautiful window of that kind which we possess.

A good example of plate tracery, which is much more abundantly used in France than in England, and apparently at an earlier period also.

Another good example of Early French work with plate tracery, it will be observed that a discharging arch is carried over the window from buttress to buttress, and that there are very few mouldings.

This example has bar tracery in the head, but the space between the circle and the heads of the lights is still solid.

In this the change to bar tracery is completed, though it is still rather clumsy; this window is more enriched with mouldings than is usual in Early French work.

	PAGE	PLATE
WINDOWS—DECORATED.		

Dorchester, Oxfordshire, c. 1300, (five examples) pls. 234, 241 — and 242

Dorchester, Oxfordshire, c. 1280 . . . 486 —

This is the east window of the north aisle, and though evidently of the same date is much earlier in character than the rest of the aisle. The mouldings (see Plate 122) are almost Early English.

Hampton Poyle, c. 1280 . . . . — ib.

A very good specimen of geometrical.

Ensham, Oxfordshire, c. 1300 . . . — 234

Solihull, Warwickshire, c. 1280 . . . — ib

This is a very curious and early example. The cusping is very peculiar, and has quite an Early English character.

Headington, Oxfordshire, c. 1320 . . . — ib

Thurning, Huntingdonshire, c. 1300 . . . — 234

An uncommon form of double lancet.

Great Haseley, Oxfordshire, c. 1300 . . . — ib

This is little more than a repetition of the last, but thrown into one by the completion of the arch and the filling the head with a quatrefoil.

Aldworth, Berkshire, c. 1300 . . . . — ib

Piddington, Oxfordshire, c. 1300 . . . — ib

A small church, but containing in the chancel many curious and interesting features. The windows are of the kind here given, they are on the intersecting principle, but being solid in the head come under the denomination of plate tracery.

Long Wittenham, Berks, c. 1280 . . . — 24

Waterperry, Oxfordshire, c. 1280 . . . — ib

Broughton, Oxfordshire, c. 1300 . : . — 24

Remarkable for the ornament of the rear arch.

Bloxham, Oxfordshire, c. 1300 . . . . — ib

GEOMETRICAL INTERSECTING TRACERY.

Northfield, Worcestershire, c. 1320 . . . — 24

A plain and good original example of this kind of tracery without foliations.

S. John's hospital, Northampton, c. 1320 . . — i

The primary tracery of this is similar to the last, but it has small arches and foliations added on the secondary plane.

	PAGE	PLATE

WINDOWS—DECORATED.

Rushden, Northamptonshire, c. 1300 . . .   —   245

The intersecting tracery of this window is concentric, that is, it is drawn from the same centres as the window arch, while in that of the preceding examples it is drawn with the same opening as the window arch but with different centres. This gives the Rushden window a strange and uneasy look.

Stanton S. John, Oxfordshire, c. 1300 . . .   —   ib.

A very uncommon example, the intersecting tracery being formed of straight lines instead of curves. It is the east window.

Stanton S. John's, Oxfordshire, c. 1300 . .   —   226

This is one of the side windows from the same beautiful chancel, and shews the trefoil-headed lancet, it also exhibits the interpenetration of the mouldings which is so common in the geometrical period.

LATE GEOMETRICAL TRACERY. Great Bedwin, Wilts, c. 1320 . . . . .   —   244

Dunchurch, Warwickshire, c. 1320 . . .   —   ib.

Shenstone, Staffordshire, c. 1350 . . .   —   ib.

Charnel chapel, Norwich, c. 1320 . . .   —   ib.

This is a very singular and unusual combination of tracery, and the arrangement of the mouldings is curious. The building is now used as the grammar school. It was built by Bishop Salmon, the foundation deed is dated 1316.

Kidlington, Oxon, c. 1320 . . . .   —   243

This shews a tendency to flowing lines.

MIXED TRACERY. Standish, Gloucestershire, c. 1350 .   —   247

Great Milton, Oxfordshire, c. 1350 . . .   —   ib.

East window, Wellingborough, Northamptonshire, c. 1300 . . . . . .   —   ib.

The tracery of this very beautiful window is a mixture of geometrical and flowing. The mouldings are very good, and the hollow is filled with rich foliage and heads. A portion of it is given on Plate 127.

Tewkesbury, Gloucestershire, c. 1320 . . .   —   239

The idea of this seems to have been taken from that of three lancets, of which the centre one is the tallest.

Bloxham, Oxfordshire, c. 1320 . . .   —   ib.

The same may be said of this.

	PAGE	PLATE

WINDOWS—DECORATED.

FLOWING TRACERY. Kingsthorpe, Northamptonshire, c. 1350 . . . . — | 236

A good example of a plain ogee-headed window, but the point terminating in a head is unusual. The tracery, by the slight alteration of changing the curved sides of the pointed oval into straight lines, becomes a very common form of a Perpendicular two-light window.

Slapton, Northamptonshire, c. 1350 . . . — | ib.

A curious combination of the ogee and semicircle.

Faringdon, Berks, c. 1320 . . . . — | 246

Another example of the ornamentation of the rear arch.

S. Mary Magdalen church, Oxford, 1318-37 . . — | ib.
Friary, Reading, A.D. 1306 . . . . — | ib.

For an account of this building, see Archæol. Journal, vol. iii. p. 141.

Higham Ferrers, Northamptonshire, c. 1350 . . — | ib.

Remarkable for the acute ogee of the window head. The same form but without foliation occurs at Finedon in the same neighbourhood.

Cranford S. Andrew's, Northamptonshire, c. 1350 . — | 248
Great Milton, Oxfordshire, c. 1350 . . . — | ib.
Slapton, Northamptonshire, c. 1350 . . . — | ib.
Melrose abbey . . . . . . — | ib.

The tracery of this window is of Flamboyant character.

S. Peter's in the East, Oxford . . . . | 162 | —
Oxford cathedral, chapel of Lady Montacute . . | 486 | —

——— (PARTLY FLAMBOYANT.) Bishop's palace chapel, Norwich, c. 1350, east window . . . . — | 249
Ditto, two side windows . . . . | 487 | —

Good examples of tracery of Flamboyant forms, though the mouldings shew they are not French work.

Raunds, Northamptonshire, c. 1350 . . . — | ib
Duston, Northamptonshire, c. 1350 . . . — | ib
Llan Tysilio, Anglesey, c. 1350 . . . — | ib
Salford, Warwickshire, c. 1360 . . . — | 25

The tracery approaches nearer to the Flamboyant in form than is usually met with in this country, but the mouldings have no resemblance to those of that style. It does not seem that genuine Flamboyant is met with in England.

	PAGE	PLAT
WINDOWS—DECORATED—CIRCULAR.		

These are very interesting and valuable examples. They are from the church of Edington which was built by Bishop Edington, the predecessor of William of Wykeham, and is therefore the earliest example of Perpendicular which we possess, though, as might be supposed, it retains much of the Decorated mixed with it. The first example appears at first sight almost pure Decorated, but on examining it, the lines which enclose the quatrefoils are seen to be straight instead of being flowing, and the upper one is of a decidedly Per-

FRONTISPIECE TO VOLUME I.

PORCH, CASTLE ASHBY CHURCH, NORTHAMPTONSHIRE.

A fine specimen of transition work from Norman to Early English.
It has been extensively repaired, or, which is more probable, rebuilt, and the jambs have suffered considerably, although a large portion of the original
work remains, and is curious; on parts of these,
small ornaments have been marked with a chisel
preparatory to carving, and one or two are in a
more advanced state, but they may be later addi-
tions; the leaves of the capitals are very simple, and of rather uncommon character; the mouldings of the arch are very
good and in fine preservation: among the enrich-
ments is a series of four-leaved flowers, formed exactly like the "tooth-ornament" of the Early English
style. This porch, together with the whole building
to which it is attached, is most carefully preserved from injury by the
noble owner of the adjoining mansion.

FRONTISPIECE TO VOLUME II.

WINDOW, CASTLE ASHBY CHURCH, NORTHAMPTONSHIRE,
   c. 1350.

PAGE PLATE

This window, which is in the west end of the north aisle, is remarkable for the elegance of its tracery. It is of Decorated character, but the mouldings, as shewn in the section, particularly of the dripstone, shew it to be rather late in the style. The other windows in the same aisle, as shewn in the Frontispiece, are of the same style and date as those of S. Mary Magdalene, Oxford (Plate 157), and consequently somewhat earlier than his.

Section of Arch of Window.

This engraving, and that of the doorway of the same church, given as a frontispiece, are presented to the work by the Most Honourable the Marquis of Northampton.

The initial letters are chiefly copied from a manuscript of the Vulgate of the 13th century, from the Canonici collection now in the Bodleian Library.

CHRONOLOGICAL TABLE.

For the use of the student Mr. Rickman's table with some slig[ht] alteration is subjoined, shewing the duration of the styles of Engli[sh] architecture, and the kings reigning in each period.

Kings.	Date.	Style.	Remarks.
William I. 1066			Prevailed little more th[an]
William II. 1087		Norman.	124 years; no remai[ns]
Henry I....................1100		[or English	really known to be mo[re]
Stephen 1135		Romanesque.]	than a few years older th[an]
Henry II.......1154 to 1189			the Conquest.
Richard I.ᵃ 1189		Early	
John.......................1199		English.	Prevailed about 100 year[s]
Henry III......1216 to 1272		[or 1st Pointed.]	
Edward I.ᵇ................1272		Decorated	Continued perhaps 10 [or]
Edward II................1307		English.	15 years later in some i[n-]
Edward III.ᶜ..1327 to 1377		[or 2nd Pointed.]	stances. Prevailed abo[ut] 100 years.
Richard II. 1377			Prevailed about 169 yea[rs]
Henry IV. 1399			
Henry V. 1413			Few, if any, whole buil[d-] ings executed in this sty[le] later than Henry VIII.
Henry VI................1422		Perpendicu-	
Edward IV...............1461		lar English.	
Edward V.................1483		[or 3rd Pointed.]	This style used in add[i-] tions and rebuilding, b[ut]
Richard III. 1483			often much debased, as la[te]
Henry VII. 1485			as 1630 or 1640.
Henry VIII....1509 to 1546			

ᵃ The reign of Richard I. was the chief period of the Transition from the Norman to the Early English style. The change began perhaps a little earlier in a few instances, and continued a little later, some buildings of the time of King John being of Transition character.

ᵇ The Transition from the Early English to the Decorated style took place chiefly in the reign of Edward I. The Eleanor crosses belong rather to the latter than the former style.

ᶜ In the latter part of the long reign of Edward III. the Transition from the Decorated to the Perpendicular style began, and was almost completed by the time of the acces-sion of Richard II. Some buildings of t[he] Decorated style may be found of his reign, b[ut] the works of William of Wykeham, We[st-] minster Hall, and many other buildings of th[at] period, are of very decided Perpendicular ch[a-] racter. Perhaps one of the earliest and b[est] authenticated examples of this Transiti[on] shewing a curious mixture of the two styl[es] is Edington church in Wiltshire, founded [by] bishop William of Edington in 1352, and co[n-] secrated in 1361. The same bishop, who d[ied] in 1366, commenced the alteration of W[in-] chester cathedral into the Perpendicular sty[le,] which was continued by William of Wykeha[m.]

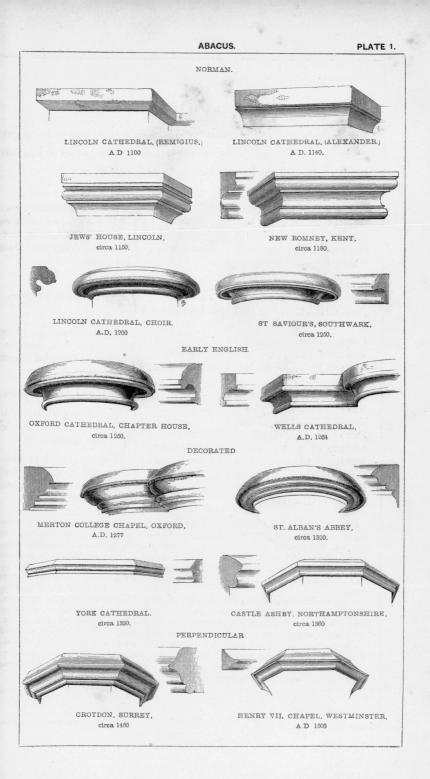

NORMAN.

LINCOLN CATHEDRAL, (REMIGIUS.)
A.D. 1100

LINCOLN CATHEDRAL, (ALEXANDER.)
A.D. 1140.

JEWS' HOUSE, LINCOLN,
circa 1150.

NEW ROMNEY, KENT,
circa 1180.

LINCOLN CATHEDRAL, CHOIR.
A.D. 1200

ST SAVIOUR'S, SOUTHWARK,
circa 1250.

EARLY ENGLISH.

OXFORD CATHEDRAL, CHAPTER HOUSE,
circa 1250.

WELLS CATHEDRAL,
A.D. 1264

DECORATED

MERTON COLLEGE CHAPEL, OXFORD,
A.D. 1277

ST. ALBAN'S ABBEY,
circa 1320.

YORK CATHEDRAL.
circa 1330.

CASTLE ASHBY, NORTHAMPTONSHIRE,
circa 1360

PERPENDICULAR

CROYDON, SURREY,
circa 1450

HENRY VII. CHAPEL, WESTMINSTER.
A.D. 1503

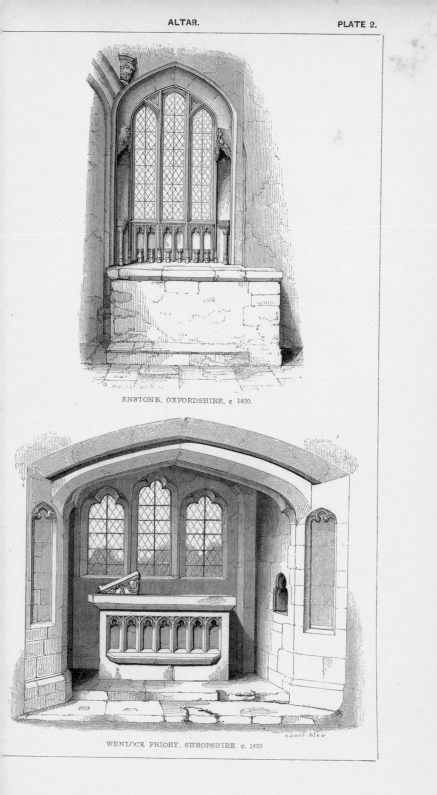

ENSTONE, OXFORDSHIRE, c 1420.

WENLOCK PRIORY, SHROPSHIRE, c. 1450.

FOULIS.

RUSHDEN, NORTHAMPTONSHIRE, c 1350.   LINCOLN CATHEDRAL.

NORMAN

DALMENY, LINLITHGOWSHIRE. c. 1150

ROMSEY, HANTS. c. 1180.

EARLY ENGLISH.

TIDMARSH, BERKSHIRE. Exterior. [The Roof and Cross are modern]

TIDMARSH, BERKSHIRE. Interior. c. 1200.

NORMAN

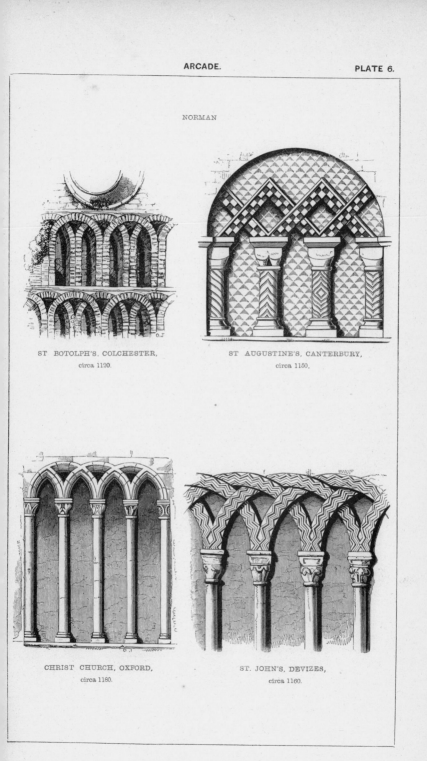

ST BOTOLPH'S, COLCHESTER,
circa 1120.

ST AUGUSTINE'S, CANTERBURY,
circa 1150.

CHRIST CHURCH, OXFORD,
circa 1180.

ST. JOHN'S, DEVIZES,
circa 1160.

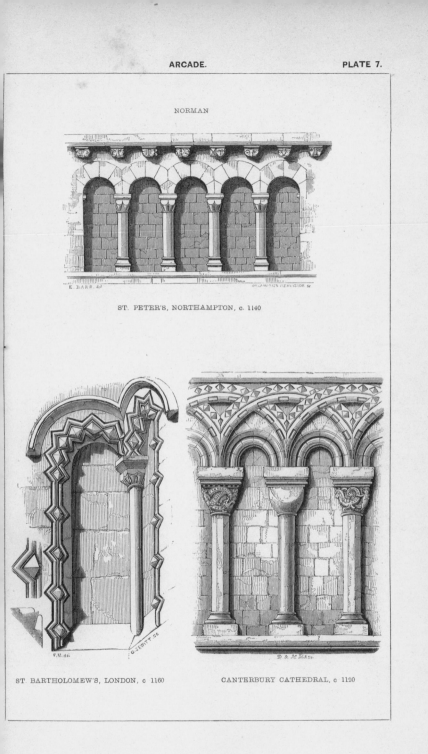

NORMAN

ST. PETER'S, NORTHAMPTON, c. 1140

ST. BARTHOLOMEW'S, LONDON, c 1160   CANTERBURY CATHEDRAL, c 1120

NORMAN

FONT, COLESHILL, WARWICKSHIRE, c. 1150.

TRANSITION.

ARCADE, STONELEIGH, WARWICKSHIRE, c. 1190

EARLY ENGLISH.

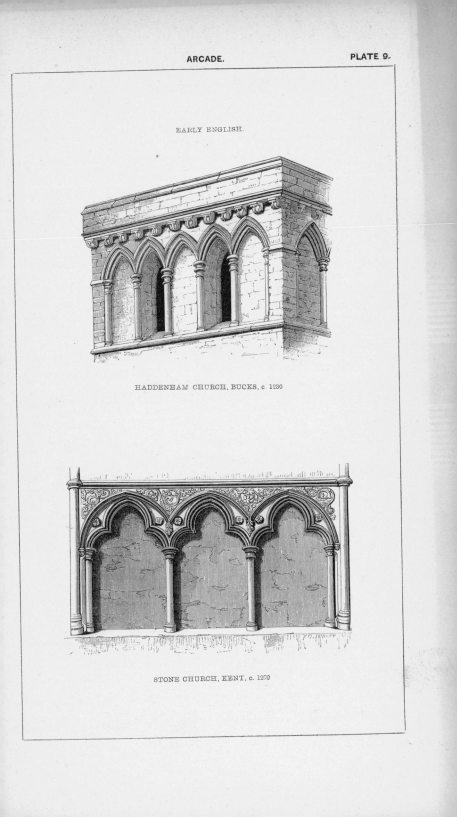

HADDENHAM CHURCH, BUCKS, c. 1230

STONE CHURCH, KENT, c. 1270

EARLY ENGLISH

SOUTH AISLE OF CHOIR, LINCOLN CATHEDRAL. c 1200.

SOUTH TRANSEPT, LINCOLN CATHEDRAL, c. 1200

DECORATED.

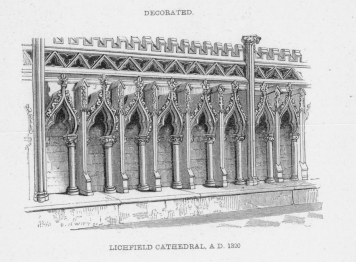

LICHFIELD CATHEDRAL, A.D. 1300

NORWICH CATHEDRAL, c. 1340

ROMAN.

ROMAN THEATRE, LILLEBONNE

ROMAN WALL, COLCHESTER, ESSEX.

NEWPORT GATE, LINCOLN

SUPPOSED SAXON

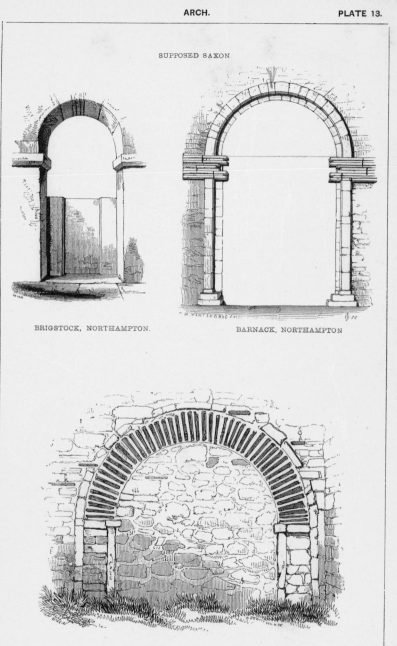

BRIGSTOCK, NORTHAMPTON.

BARNACK, NORTHAMPTON

BRITFORD, NEAR SALISBURY

EARLY NORMAN

CHAPEL IN THE WHITE TOWER, LONDON,
A.D 1081

WEST END OF LINCOLN CATHEDRAL,
circa 1090

GREAT MALVERN, WORCESTERSHIRE, c 1100.

NORMAN.

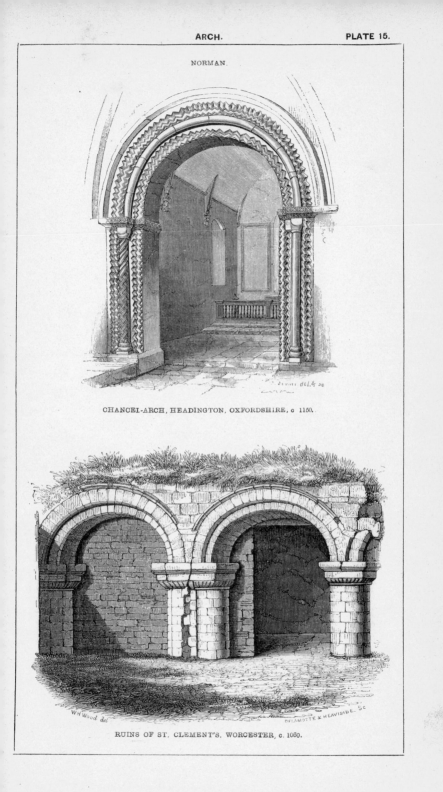

CHANCEL-ARCH, HEADINGTON, OXFORDSHIRE, c 1150.

RUINS OF ST. CLEMENT'S, WORCESTER, c. 1060.

TRANSITION FROM NORMAN

GALILEE, DURHAM CATHEDRAL, A.D. 1188.

FOUNTAINS ABBEY, c 1180

EARLY ENGLISH.

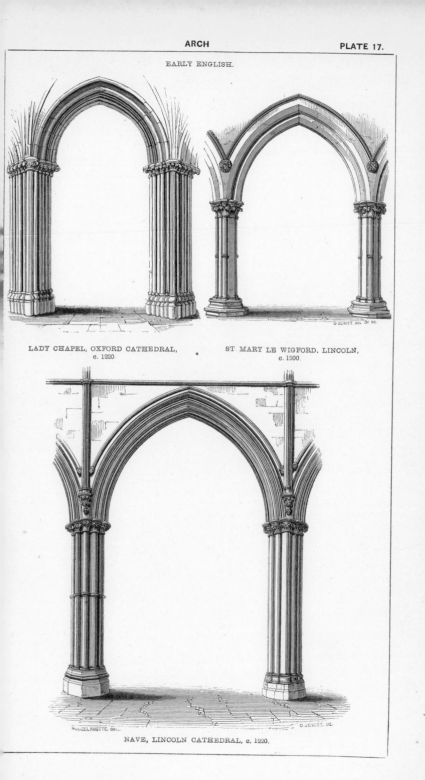

LADY CHAPEL, OXFORD CATHEDRAL,
c. 1220.

ST. MARY LE WIGFORD. LINCOLN,
c. 1200.

NAVE, LINCOLN CATHEDRAL, c. 1220.

DECORATED.

CHIPPING WARDEN, NORTHAMPTONSHIRE. c. 1350

HOWDEN CHURCH, YORKSHIRE, c. 1350.

DECORATED.

O. JEWITT del et sc

DORCHESTER, OXFORDSHIRE, c. 1300

PERPENDICULAR.

NAVE OF ST. MARY'S, OXFORD, A.D. 1488.   SHERBORNE, DORSETSHIRE, A.D. 1490.

MINSTER LOVELL, OXFORDSHIRE, c. 1430.

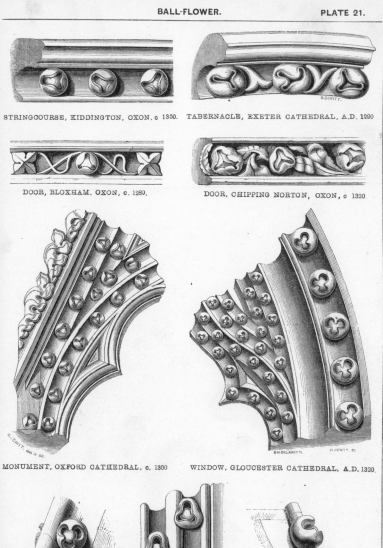

STRINGCOURSE, KIDDINGTON, OXON, c 1350.

TABERNACLE, EXETER CATHEDRAL, A.D. 1290

DOOR, BLOXHAM, OXON, c. 1280.

DOOR, CHIPPING NORTON, OXON, c 1320

MONUMENT, OXFORD CATHEDRAL, c. 1300

WINDOW, GLOUCESTER CATHEDRAL, A.D. 1320.

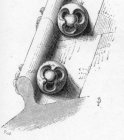

SPIRE, SALISBURY
CATHEDRAL, c 1300.

WINDOW JAMB, OXFORD
CATHEDRAL, c. 1320.

SPIRE, SALISBURY
CATHEDRAL, c. 1300.

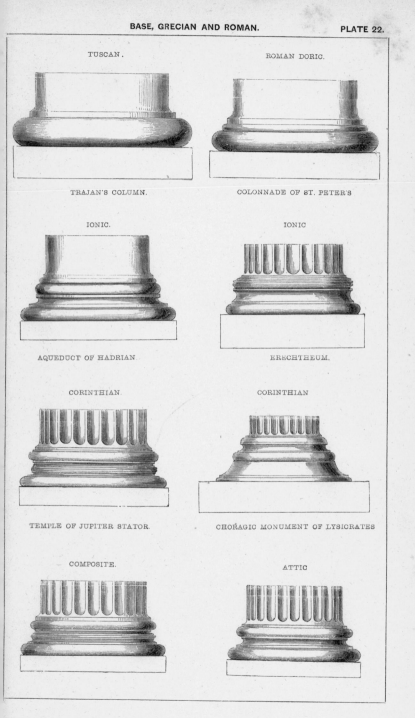

TUSCAN.

ROMAN DORIC.

TRAJAN'S COLUMN.

COLONNADE OF ST. PETER'S

IONIC.

IONIC

AQUEDUCT OF HADRIAN.

ERECHTHEUM.

CORINTHIAN.

CORINTHIAN

TEMPLE OF JUPITER STATOR.

CHORAGIC MONUMENT OF LYSICRATES

COMPOSITE.

ATTIC

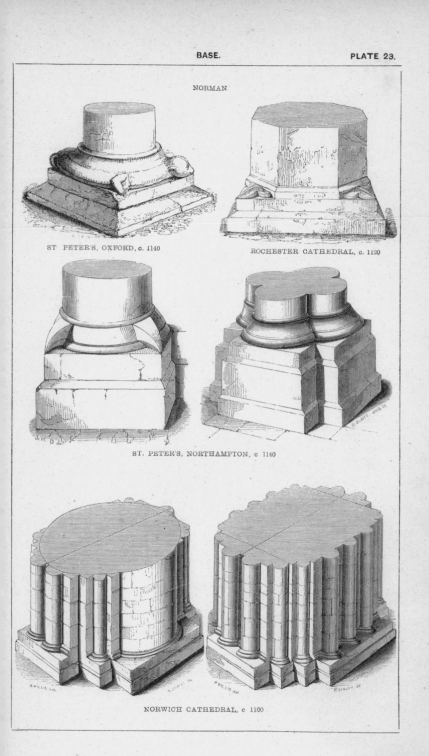

NORMAN

ST PETER'S, OXFORD, c. 1140

ROCHESTER CATHEDRAL, c. 1120

ST. PETER'S, NORTHAMPTON, c 1140

NORWICH CATHEDRAL, c 1100

EARLY ENGLISH.

GREAT HASELEY, OXFORDSHIRE, c 1200.

ST. ALBAN'S ABBEY, c. 1250.

CANTERBURY CATHEDRAL, A.D. 1178.

CHAPTER HOUSE, LINCOLN, c. 1200.

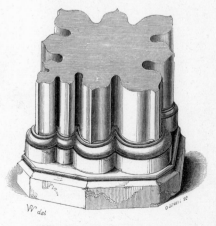

EMPLE CHURCH LONDON, A.D 1240.

ST. MARY S ABBEY, YORK, c. 1250.

DECORATED.

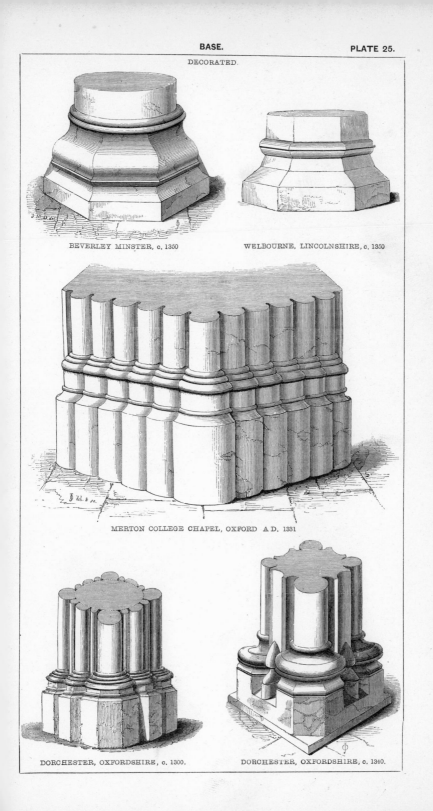

BEVERLEY MINSTER, c. 1350

WELBOURNE, LINCOLNSHIRE, c. 1350

MERTON COLLEGE CHAPEL, OXFORD A.D. 1331

DORCHESTER, OXFORDSHIRE, c. 1300.

DORCHESTER, OXFORDSHIRE, c. 1340.

PERPENDICULAR

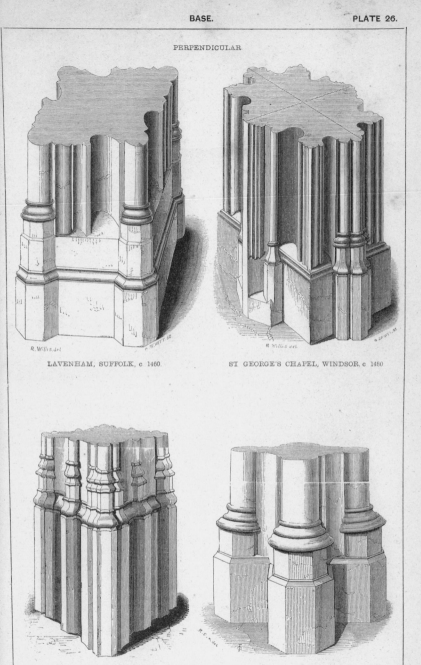

LAVENHAM, SUFFOLK, c 1460.

ST GEORGE'S CHAPEL, WINDSOR, c 1480

ST. MARY'S, OXFORD, 1488

CROYDON, SURREY, circa 1450.

CRYPT, YORK CATHEDRAL, c. 1160

STOCKBURY, KENT, c. 1220.

ST CROSS, WINCHESTER. c 1180

CANTERBURY CATHEDRAL, c. 1180.

SALISBURY CATHEDRAL, c. 1230.

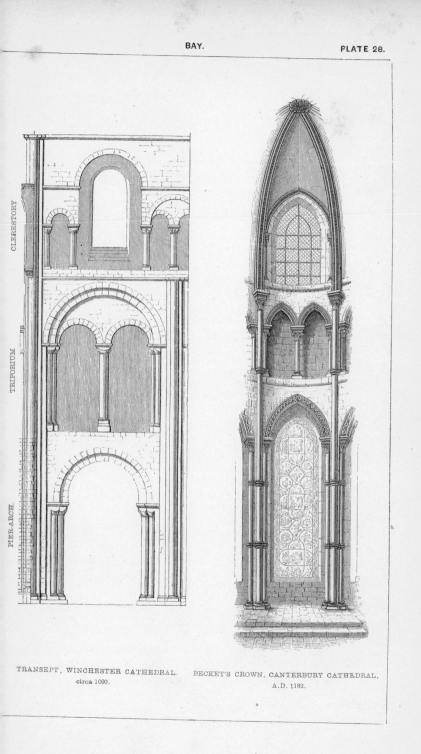

TRANSEPT, WINCHESTER CATHEDRAL.
circa 1090.

BECKET'S CROWN, CANTERBURY CATHEDRAL.
A.D. 1182.

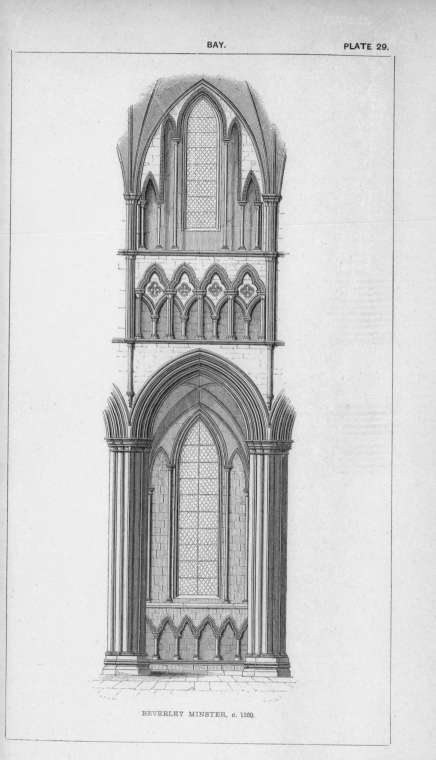

BEVERLEY MINSTER, c. 1250.

THORNTON ABBEY, LINCOLNSHIRE, c. 1282.

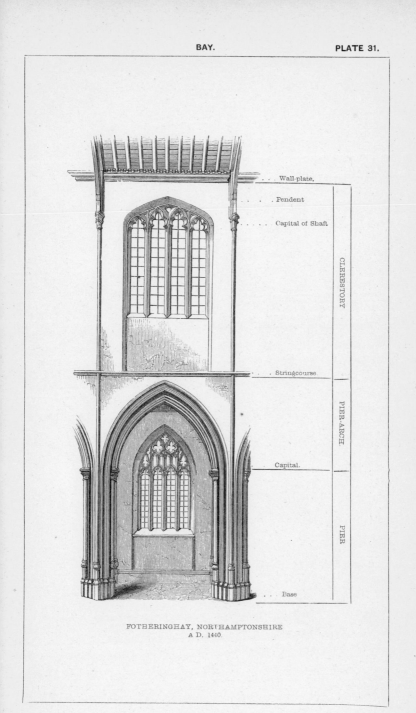

Wall-plate.

Pendent

Capital of Shaft

CLERESTORY

Stringcourse.

PIER-ARCH.

Capital.

PIER

Base

FOTHERINGHAY, NORTHAMPTONSHIRE
A.D. 1440.

NORMAN.

LITTLETON, HAMPSHIRE

NORTHBOROUGH, NORTHAMPTONSHIRE

EARLY ENGLISH.

MANTON, RUTLAND

LITTLE CASTERTON, RUTLAND.

EARLY ENGLISH

LITTLE COXWELL, BERKSHIRE
c. 1200.

SKELTON, YORKSHIRE, c 1220.

CHAPEL, GLASTONBURY,
circa 1250

SHIPTON OLLIFFE, GLOUCESTERSHIRE,
circa 1260

EARLY ENGLISH

PERPENDICULAR

LEIGH DELAMERE, WILTS, c. 1250.

CORSTON, WILTS, c. 1440.

DECORATED

IDBURY, OXFORDSHIRE. c. 1450.

CLEEVE ABBEY. SOMERSET c. 1320.

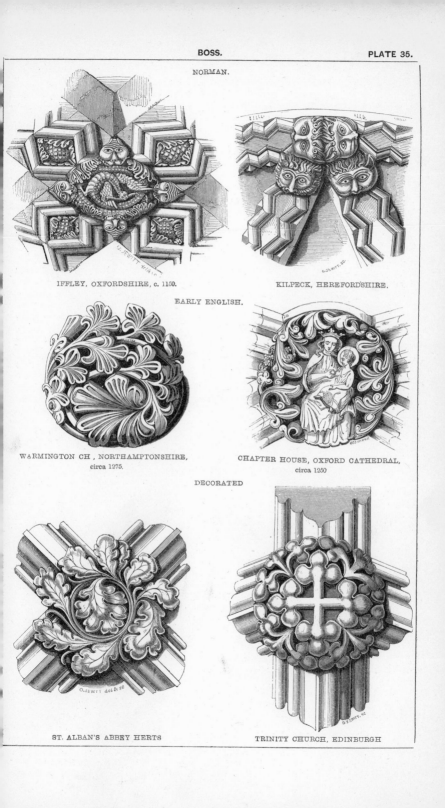

NORMAN.

IFFLEY, OXFORDSHIRE, c. 1150.

KILPECK, HEREFORDSHIRE.

EARLY ENGLISH.

WARMINGTON CH., NORTHAMPTONSHIRE,
circa 1275.

CHAPTER HOUSE, OXFORD CATHEDRAL,
circa 1250

DECORATED

ST. ALBAN'S ABBEY HERTS

TRINITY CHURCH, EDINBURGH

PERPENDICULAR.

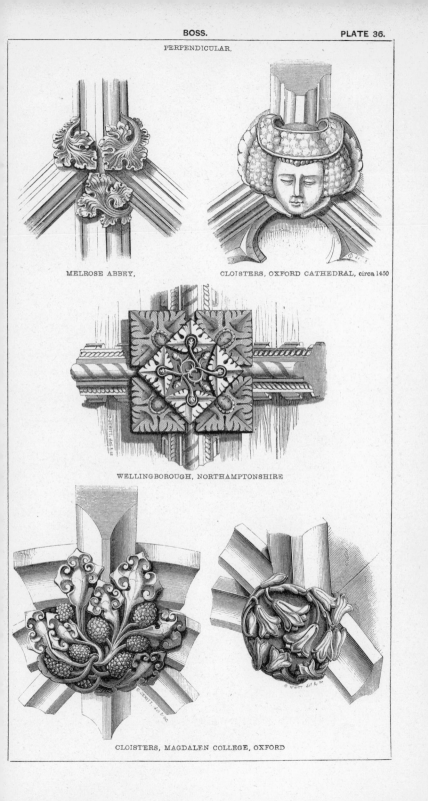

MELROSE ABBEY.   CLOISTERS, OXFORD CATHEDRAL, circa 1450.

WELLINGBOROUGH, NORTHAMPTONSHIRE.

CLOISTERS, MAGDALEN COLLEGE, OXFORD.

NORMAN

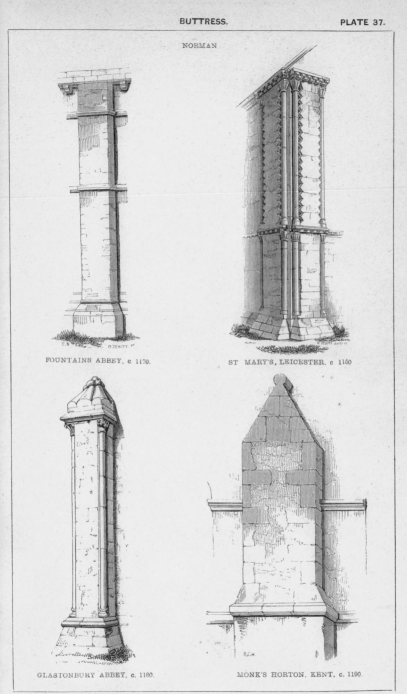

FOUNTAINS ABBEY, c. 1170.

ST MARY'S, LEICESTER, c 1150

GLASTONBURY ABBEY, c. 1180.

MONK'S HORTON, KENT, c. 1190.

EARLY ENGLISH.

CHOIR, LINCOLN, c 1190.

EARLY ENGLISH.

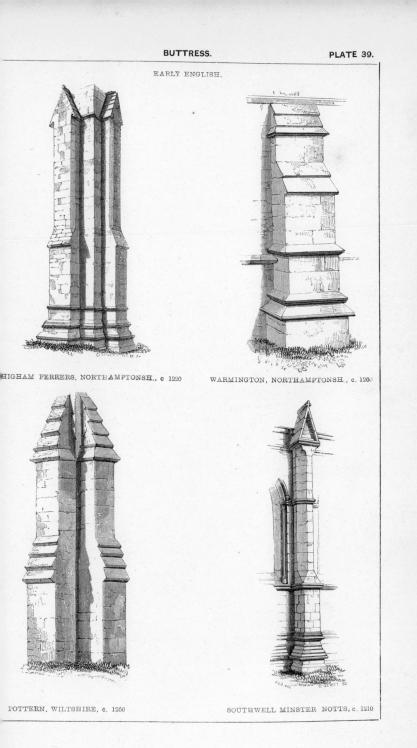

HIGHAM FERRERS, NORTHAMPTONSH., c 1220

WARMINGTON, NORTHAMPTONSH., c. 1260

POTTERN, WILTSHIRE, c. 1250

SOUTHWELL MINSTER NOTTS, c. 1210

DECORATED.

DORCHESTER, OXFORDSHIRE,
c. 1300.

BRINGTON, NORTHAMPTONSH.,
c 1320.

OXFORD CATHEDRAL.

CHURCH BRAMPTON, NORTHANTS

ST MARY MAGDALENE, OXFORD,
A D 1337

GADSBY, LEICESTERSHIRE,
c 1350.

PERPENDICULAR

WELLINGBOROUGH,
NORTHAMPTONSHIRE, c 1450

GLOUCESTER CATHEDRAL,
circa 1430.

ST. LAURENCE,
EVESHAM, circa 1450

DIVINITY SCHOOL,
OXFORD, c 1490.

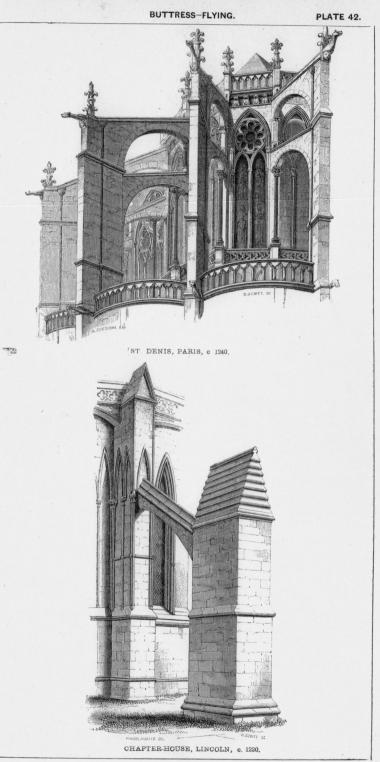

ST. DENIS, PARIS, c 1240.

CHAPTER-HOUSE, LINCOLN, c. 1220.

PERPENDICULAR

FOTHERINGHAY, NORTHAMPTONSHIRE,
A.D. 1440.

PERPENDICULAR.   DECORATED.

SHERBORNE, DORSETSHIRE,   CAYTHORPE, LINCOLNSHIRE,
circa 1470   circa 1320.

ROMAN DORIC.   GRECIAN DORIC

ROMAN IONIC   GRECIAN IONIC

CORINTHIAN,   COMPOSITE.

NORMAN.

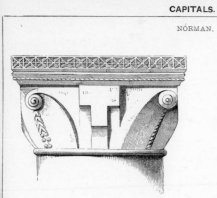

WHITE TOWER, LONDON, c. 1080

WESTMINSTER HALL, c 1090

ST NICOLAS, CAEN, c 1100.

LINCOLN CATHEDRAL, c. 1100

WHITBY PARISH CHURCH, c. 1100

CANTERBURY CATHEDRAL, CRYPT

NORMAN.

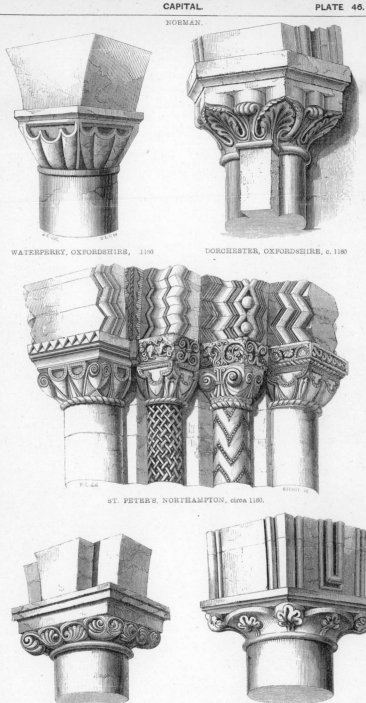

WATERPERRY, OXFORDSHIRE, 1180   DORCHESTER, OXFORDSHIRE, c. 1180

ST. PETER'S, NORTHAMPTON, circa 1160.

GRAFTON UNDERWOOD, NORTHAMPTONSHIRE, c. 1180   HASELEY, OXFORDSHIRE, c. 1200

ENGLISH TRANSITION

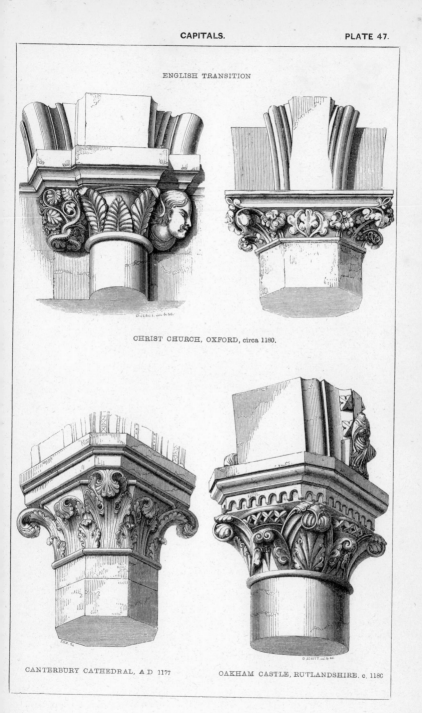

CHRIST CHURCH, OXFORD, circa 1180.

CANTERBURY CATHEDRAL, A.D. 1177   OAKHAM CASTLE, RUTLANDSHIRE. c. 1180

NORMAN

FOREIGN TRANSITION

MURRHARD, c. 1188

SOISSONS CATHEDRAL, A.D. 1212.

ST NICOLAS, BLOIS, c 1200

ST NICOLAS, BLOIS, c. 1200

EARLY ENGLISH

BURTON LATIMER, NORTHAMPTONSHIRE, c 1190

BLOXHAM, OXFORDSHIRE, c. 1190.

WOODFORD, NORTHAMPTONSHIRE, c 1190

NASEBY, NORTHAMPTONSHIRE, c. 1220.

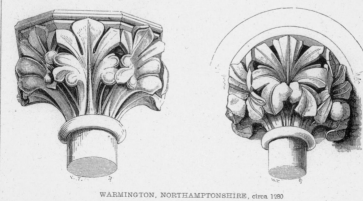

WARMINGTON, NORTHAMPTONSHIRE, circa 1280

EARLY ENGLISH

CHOIR, LINCOLN CATHEDRAL, c 1200

PRESBYTERY, LINCOLN CATHEDRAL, c 1260

ST. MARY LE WIGFORD, LINCOLN, c. 1200.

DESBOROUGH, NORTHAMPTONSHIRE, c. 1220.

DECORATED

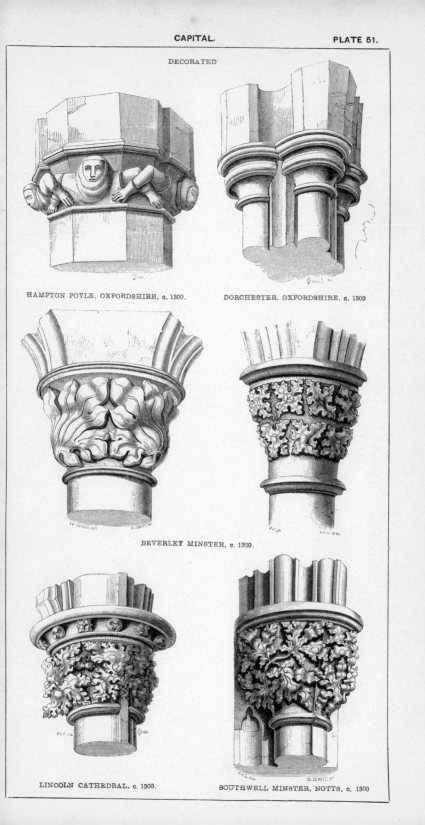

HAMPTON POYLE, OXFORDSHIRE, c. 1300.

DORCHESTER, OXFORDSHIRE, c. 1300.

BEVERLEY MINSTER, c. 1300.

LINCOLN CATHEDRAL, c. 1300.

SOUTHWELL MINSTER, NOTTS, c. 1300.

PERPENDICULAR

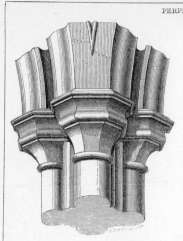

WELLINGBOROUGH, NORTHANTS, c. 1450.

NEWARK, NOTTINGHAMSHIRE, c. 1380.

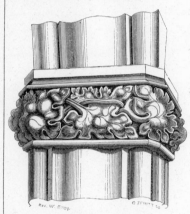

STOKE IN TEIGNHEAD, DEVONSH., c. 1480

CROMER, NORFOLK, c 1420.

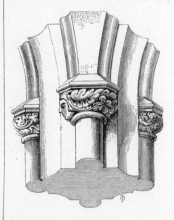

PIDDLETON, DORSETSHIRE, A.D. 1505.

UPWEY, DORSETSHIRE, c. 1500.

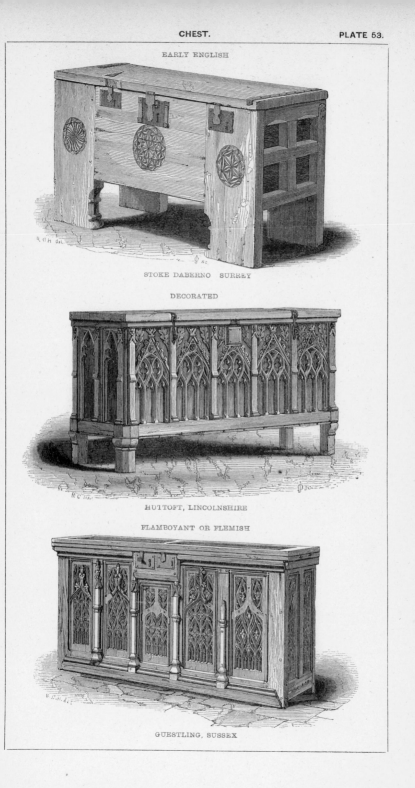

EARLY ENGLISH

STOKE DABERNO SURREY

DECORATED

HUTTOFT, LINCOLNSHIRE

FLAMBOYANT OR FLEMISH

GUESTLING, SUSSEX

ABINGDON ABBEY, BERKS,
circa 1250

AYDON CASTLE, NORTHUMBERLAND,
circa 1280

SHERBORNE ABBEY, DORSET,
circa 1300

EXTON, RUTLAND.
circa 1350.

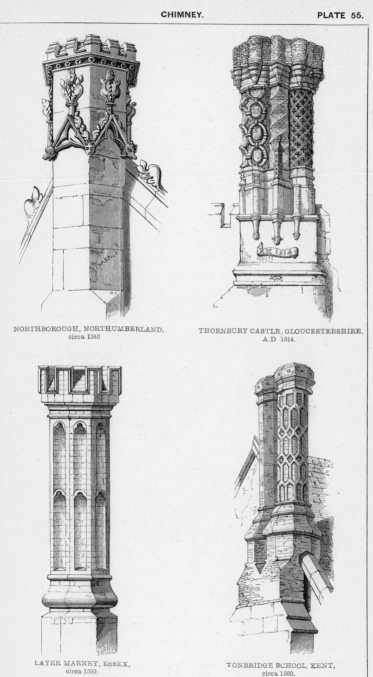

NORTHBOROUGH, NORTHUMBERLAND,
circa 1340

THORNBURY CASTLE, GLOUCESTERSHIRE,
A.D 1514.

LAYER MARNEY, ESSEX,
circa 1530.

TONBRIDGE SCHOOL, KENT,
circa 1560.

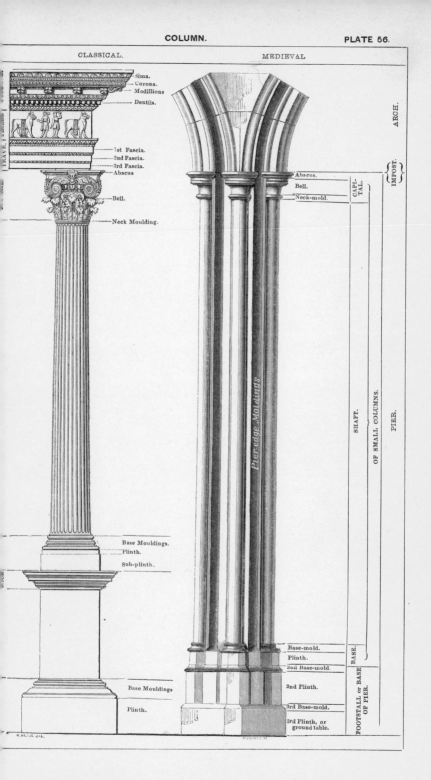

CLASSICAL.   MEDIEVAL

Sima.
Corona.
Modillions.
Dentils.

1st Fascia.
2nd Fascia.
3rd Fascia.
Abacus

Bell.

Neck Moulding.

Base Mouldings.
Plinth.
Sub-plinth.

Base Mouldings
Plinth.

ARCH.

Abacus.
Bell.
Neck-mold.

IMPOST.

CAPITAL.

Pier-edge Moldings

SHAFT.
OF SMALL COLUMNS.

PIER.

Base-mold.
Plinth.
2nd Base-mold.
2nd Plinth.
3rd Base-mold.
3rd Plinth, or
ground table.

BASE.

FOOTSTALL or BASE
OF PIER.

NORMAN.   TRANSITION

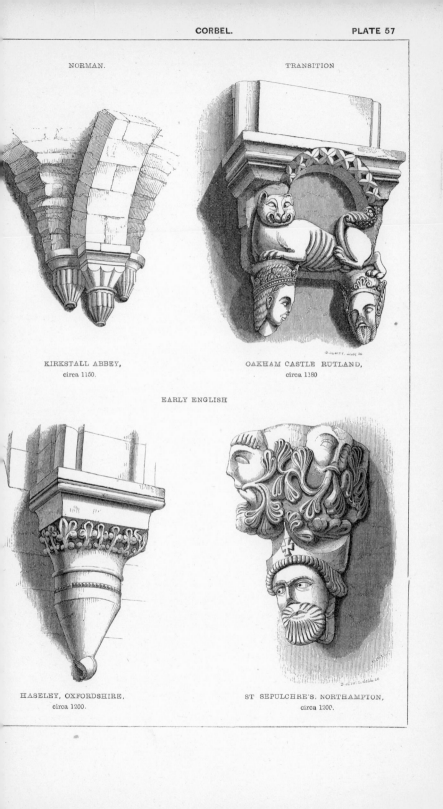

KIRKSTALL ABBEY,
circa 1150.

OAKHAM CASTLE RUTLAND,
circa 1180

EARLY ENGLISH

HASELEY, OXFORDSHIRE,
circa 1200.

ST SEPULCHRE'S. NORTHAMPTON,
circa 1200.

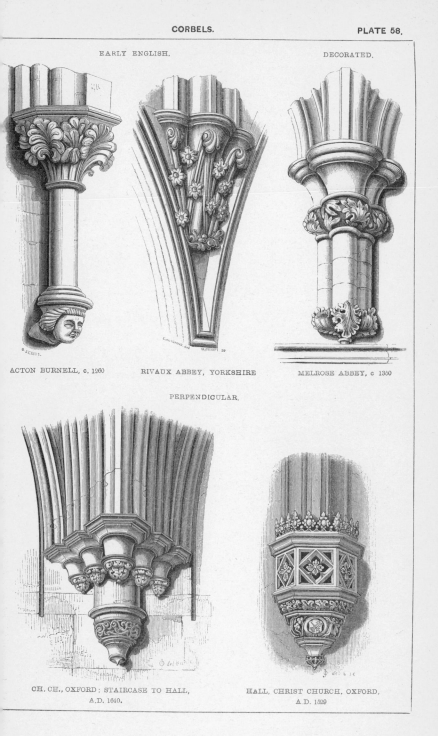

EARLY ENGLISH.

DECORATED.

ACTON BURNELL, c. 1260

RIVAUX ABBEY, YORKSHIRE

MELROSE ABBEY, c 1350

PERPENDICULAR.

CH. CH., OXFORD; STAIRCASE TO HALL,
A.D. 1640.

HALL, CHRIST CHURCH, OXFORD,
A.D. 1529

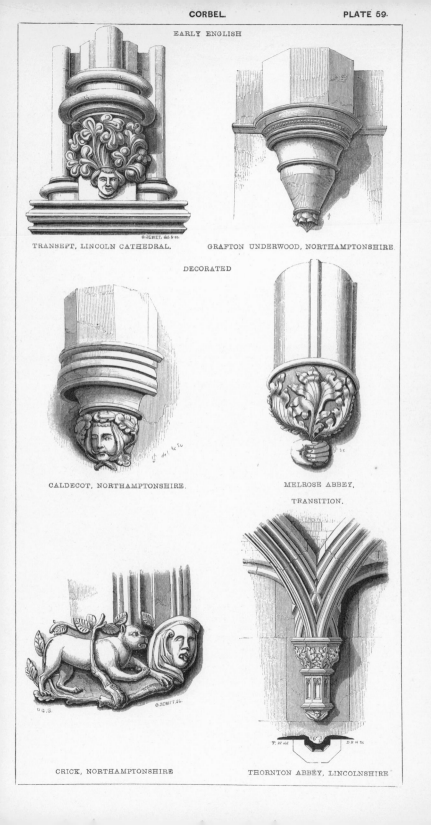

EARLY ENGLISH

TRANSEPT, LINCOLN CATHEDRAL.

GRAFTON UNDERWOOD, NORTHAMPTONSHIRE.

DECORATED

CALDECOT, NORTHAMPTONSHIRE.

MELROSE ABBEY.

TRANSITION.

CRICK, NORTHAMPTONSHIRE

THORNTON ABBEY, LINCOLNSHIRE

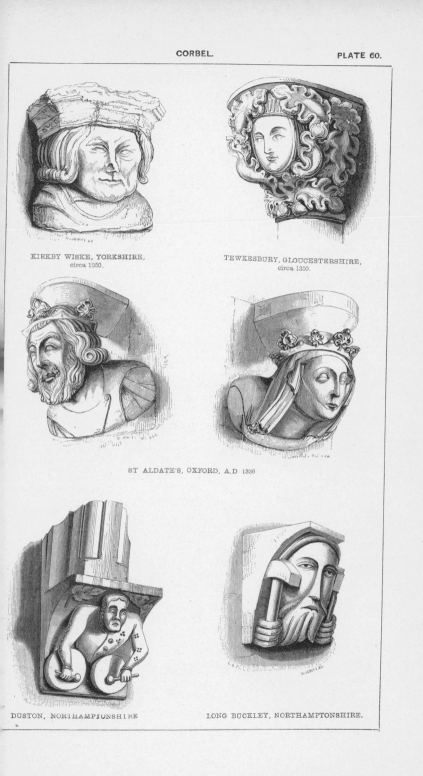

KIRKBY WISKE, YORKSHIRE,
circa 1250.

TEWKESBURY, GLOUCESTERSHIRE,
circa 1350.

ST ALDATE'S, OXFORD, A.D 1336

DUSTON, NORTHAMPTONSHIRE

LONG BUCKLEY, NORTHAMPTONSHIRE.

WELLS CATHEDRAL. c 1250.

NORTHMOOR CHURCH, OXON, c. 1320

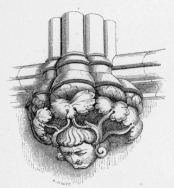

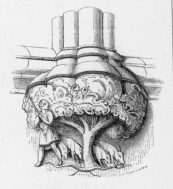

MERTON COLLEGE CHAPEL, OXFORD, A.D. 1277.

ST MARY'S CHURCH, OXFORD, A.D. 1488.

YORK CATHEDRAL, c. 1450

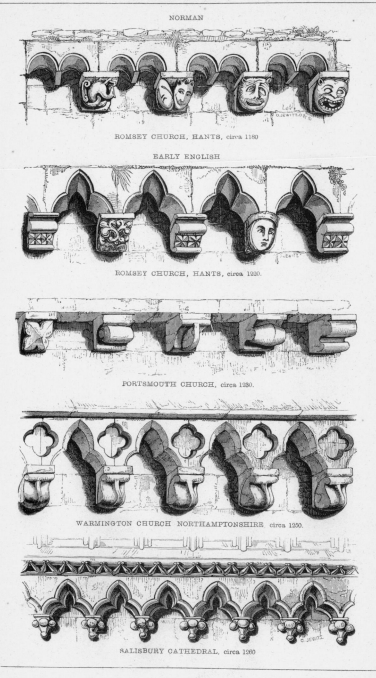

NORMAN

ROMSEY CHURCH, HANTS, circa 1180

EARLY ENGLISH

ROMSEY CHURCH, HANTS, circa 1220.

PORTSMOUTH CHURCH, circa 1230.

WARMINGTON CHURCH NORTHAMPTONSHIRE, circa 1250.

SALISBURY CATHEDRAL, circa 1260

DECORATED.

TOWER OF ST MARY'S, OXFORD, circa 1280

CHANCEL OF GRANTHAM, LINCOLNSHIRE, circa 1320.

PERPENDICULAR.

ENSHAM CHURCH, OXON, circa 1450.

BISHOP BECKINGTON'S CHANTRY, WELLS CATHEDRAL, A D 1465

GATEWAY OF THE CLOSE, WELLS, A D 1505

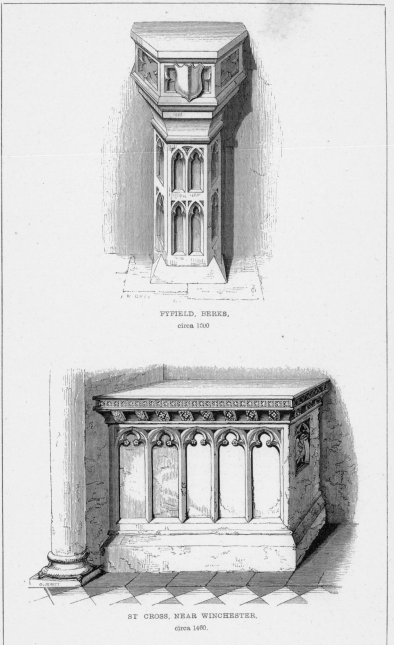

FYFIELD, BERKS,
circa 1500

ST CROSS, NEAR WINCHESTER,
circa 1460.

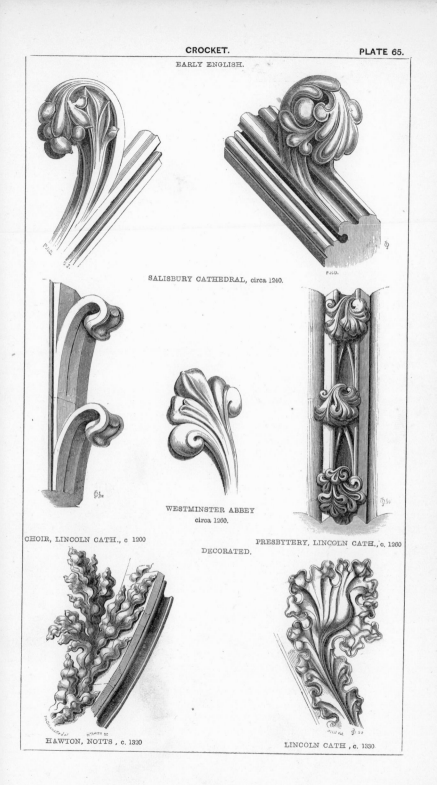

EARLY ENGLISH.

SALISBURY CATHEDRAL, circa 1240.

WESTMINSTER ABBEY
circa 1260.

CHOIR, LINCOLN CATH., c 1200

PRESBYTERY, LINCOLN CATH., c. 1260

DECORATED.

HAWTON, NOTTS, c. 1330

LINCOLN CATH, c. 1330

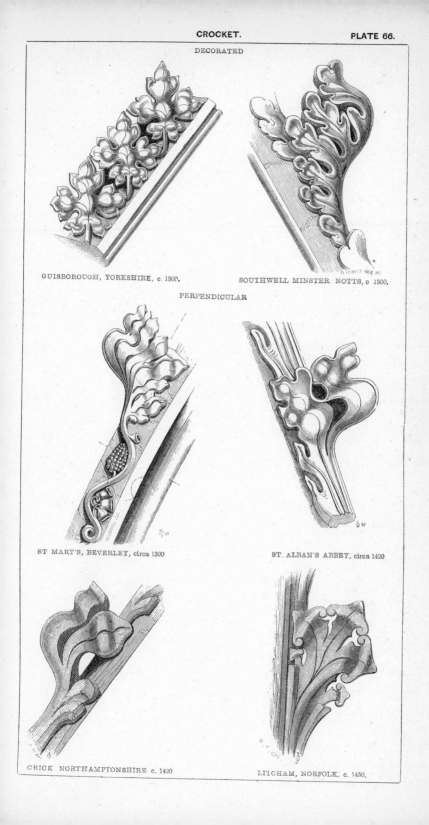

DECORATED

GUISBOROUGH, YORKSHIRE, c. 1300.

SOUTHWELL MINSTER. NOTTS, c 1300.

PERPENDICULAR

ST MARY'S, BEVERLEY, circa 1390

ST. ALBAN'S ABBEY, circa 1420

CRICK NORTHAMPTONSHIRE c. 1420

LITCHAM, NORFOLK, c. 1450.

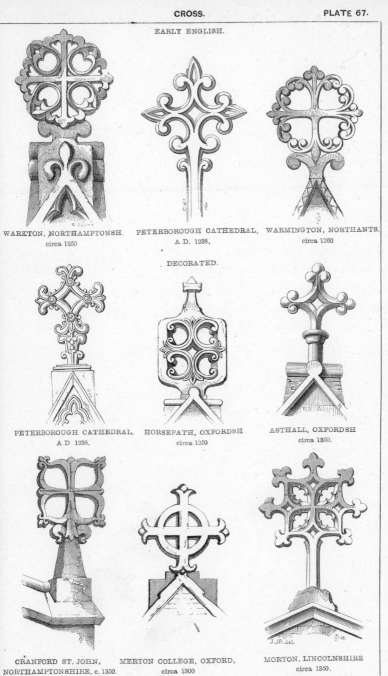

EARLY ENGLISH.

WARKTON, NORTHAMPTONSH.
circa 1250

PETERBOROUGH CATHEDRAL,
A.D. 1238.

WARMINGTON, NORTHANTS.
circa 1260

DECORATED.

PETERBOROUGH CATHEDRAL,
A.D. 1238.

HORSEPATH, OXFORDSH
circa 1250

ASTHALL, OXFORDSH
circa 1350.

CRANFORD ST. JOHN,
NORTHAMPTONSHIRE, c. 1350.

MERTON COLLEGE, OXFORD,
circa 1300

MORTON, LINCOLNSHIRE
circa 1350.

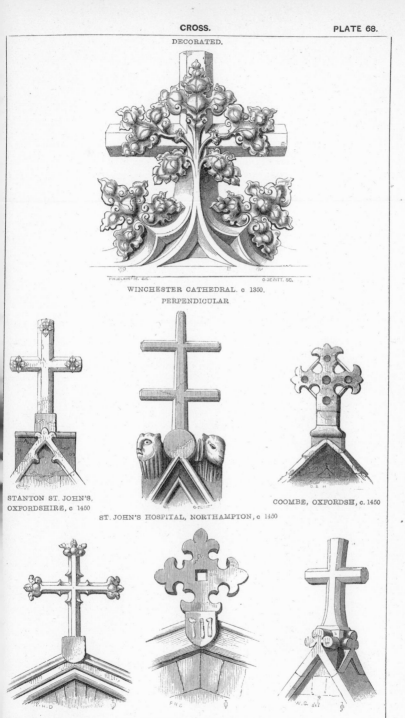

DECORATED.

WINCHESTER CATHEDRAL. c 1350.

PERPENDICULAR

STANTON ST. JOHN'S.
OXFORDSHIRE, c 1450

ST. JOHN'S HOSPITAL, NORTHAMPTON, c 1450

COOMBE, OXFORDSH, c. 1450

ROTHERHAM, YORKSHIRE, c. 1450   ECCLESFIELD, YORKSHIRE, c 1500   PINHOE, DEVON, c. 1450

NORMAN   EARLY ENGLISH.

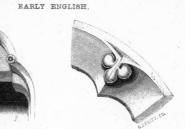

ELY CATHEDRAL   NUN MONKTON, YORKSHIRE,   HIGHAM FERRERS,
                                 c. 1200   NORTHAMPTONSHIRE, c. 1220

PRESTON, YORKSHIRE.   RAUNDS, NORTHAMPTONSHIRE, c 1220

PRESBYTERY, LINCOLN CATHEDRAL, c. 1260.

LATE DECORATED.

PRESBYTERY, LINCOLN CATHEDRAL, c 1260.   LINCOLN CATHEDRAL, c. 1380.

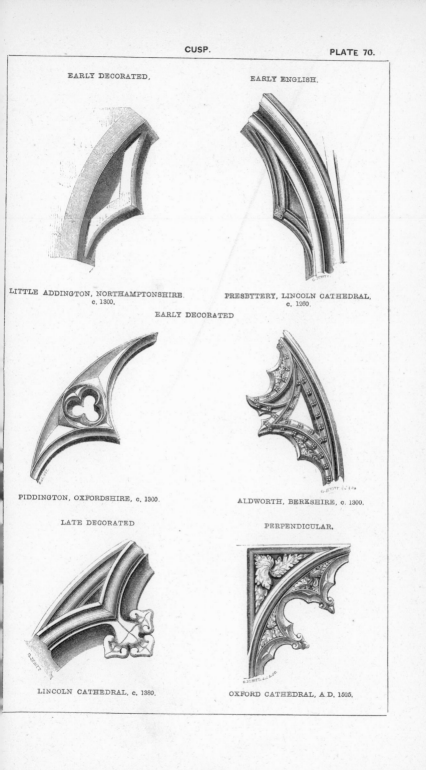

EARLY DECORATED.

EARLY ENGLISH.

LITTLE ADDINGTON, NORTHAMPTONSHIRE.
c. 1300.

PRESBYTERY, LINCOLN CATHEDRAL,
c. 1260.

EARLY DECORATED

PIDDINGTON, OXFORDSHIRE, c. 1300.

ALDWORTH, BERKSHIRE, c. 1300.

LATE DECORATED

PERPENDICULAR.

LINCOLN CATHEDRAL, c. 1380.

OXFORD CATHEDRAL, A.D. 1525.

NORMAN

ESSENDINE CHAPEL, RUTLAND
circa 1130.

ST. MARGARET'S-AT-CLIFFE, DOVER,
circa 1130.

NORMAN

ST. EBBE'S CHURCH, OXFORD,
circa 1140

IFFLEY CHURCH, OXFORDSHIRE
circa 1140

NORMAN.

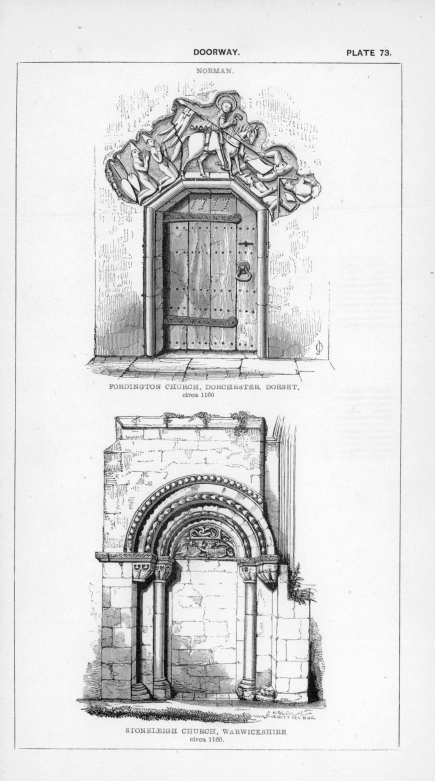

FORDINGTON CHURCH, DORCHESTER, DORSET,
circa 1160.

STONELEIGH CHURCH, WARWICKSHIRE.
circa 1160.

NORMAN

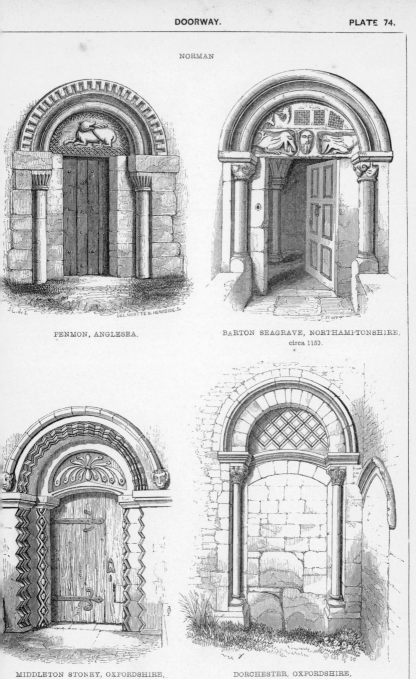

PENMON, ANGLESEA.

BARTON SEAGRAVE, NORTHAMPTONSHIRE,
circa 1150.

MIDDLETON STONEY, OXFORDSHIRE,
circa 1150

DORCHESTER, OXFORDSHIRE,
circa 1160

NORMAN

FRITWELL, OXFORDSHIRE,
circa 1150

KIRKHAM PRIORY, YORKSHIRE,
circa 1150

NEWINGTON, OXFORDSHIRE,
circa 1160

CUDDESDEN, OXFORDSHIRE,
circa 1160

EARLY ENGLISH.

LUTTON, HUNTINGDONSHIRE,
circa 1200,

BURTON LATIMER, NORTHAMPTONSHIRE.

WARMINGTON, NORTHAMPTONSHIRE,
circa 1260

EARLY ENGLISH

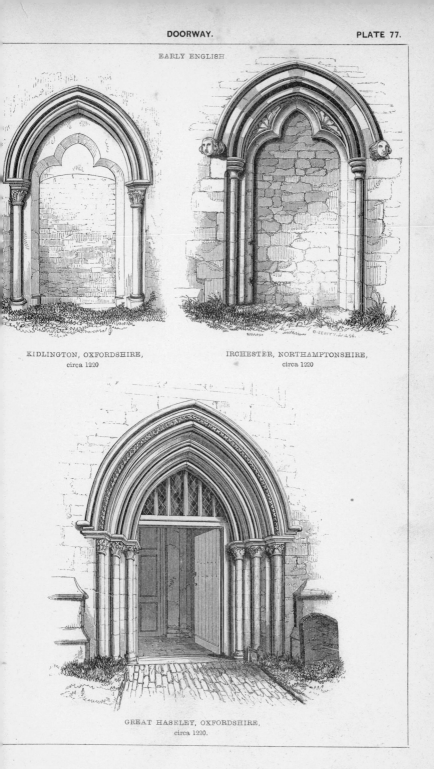

KIDLINGTON, OXFORDSHIRE,
circa 1220

IRCHESTER, NORTHAMPTONSHIRE,
circa 1220

GREAT HASELEY, OXFORDSHIRE,
circa 1220.

EARLY ENGLISH.

AYLESBURY, BUCKINGHAMSHIRE, c. 1250

HEYTESBURY, WILTS. c. 1220.   WOODFORD, NORTHAMPTONSHIRE, c. 1250

PLATE IX.

LICHFIELD CATHEDRAL, c. 1260.

DECORATED.

MILTON KEYNES, BUCKINGHAMSHIRE, c 1320.   CANTERBURY CATHEDRAL, A D. 1304.

DECORATED.

BANBURY, OXFORDSHIRE.
circa 1350

DUNCHURCH, WARWICKSHIRE,
circa 1350

PERPENDICULAR

MERTON COLLEGE CHAPEL, OXFORD,
A.D. 1424

FOTHERINGHAY, NORTHAMPTONSHIRE,
A.D. 1440

PERPENDICULAR,

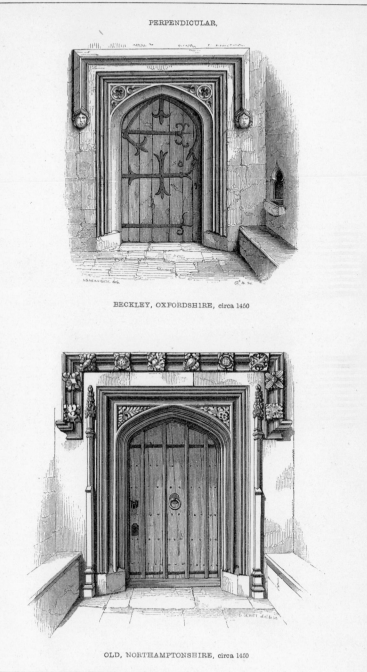

BECKLEY, OXFORDSHIRE, circa 1450

OLD, NORTHAMPTONSHIRE, circa 1450

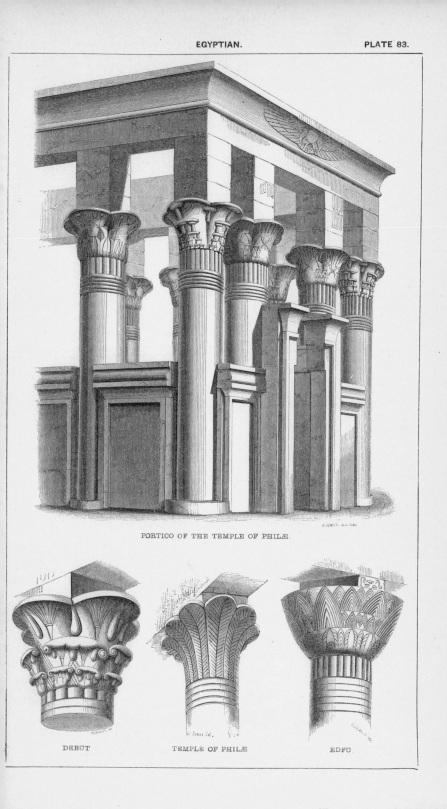

PORTICO OF THE TEMPLE OF PHILÆ.

DEBUT   TEMPLE OF PHILÆ   EDFU

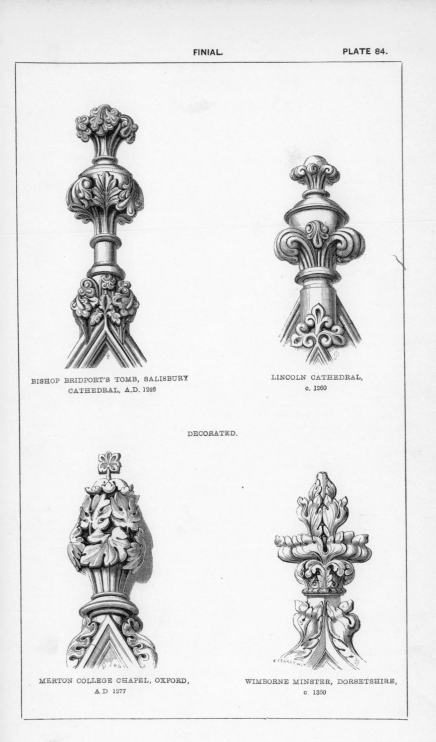

BISHOP BRIDPORT'S TOMB, SALISBURY
CATHEDRAL, A.D. 1246

LINCOLN CATHEDRAL,
c. 1260

DECORATED.

MERTON COLLEGE CHAPEL, OXFORD,
A.D 1277

WIMBORNE MINSTER, DORSETSHIRE,
c. 1350

DECORATED.

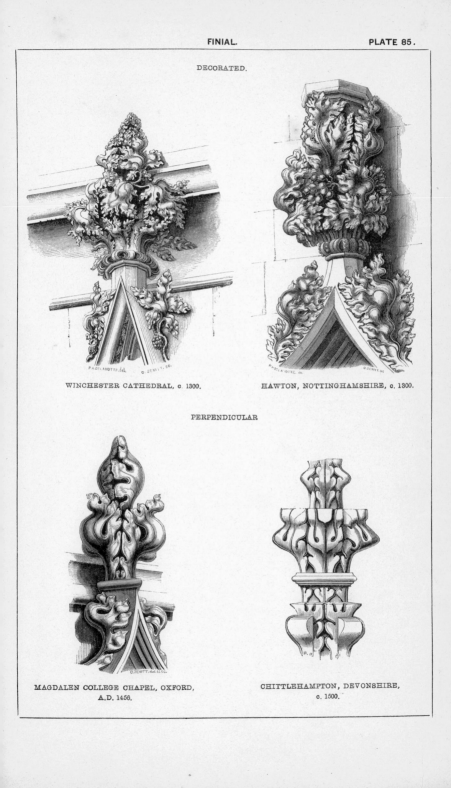

WINCHESTER CATHEDRAL, c. 1300.

HAWTON, NOTTINGHAMSHIRE, c. 1300.

PERPENDICULAR

MAGDALEN COLLEGE CHAPEL, OXFORD,
A.D. 1456.

CHITTLEHAMPTON, DEVONSHIRE,
c. 1500.

NORTHBOROUGH, c. 1320

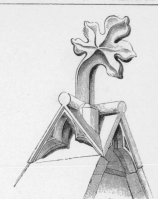

BARN, BATH HAMPTON, c. 1350

BARN, BATH HAMPTON, c. 1350

WOLVERTON HALL, DORSET, c. 1500

SHREWSBURY, c. 1580.

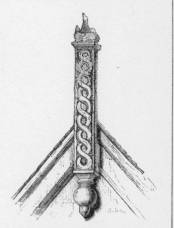

CASTLE INN, CAMBRIDGE, c 1620

NORMAN.

ROCHESTER CASTLE, circa 1130.

CONISBOROUGH CASTLE, circa 1170.

EARLY ENGLISH.

AYDON CASTLE, NORTHUMBERLAND, circa 1270.

EARLY ENGLISH.

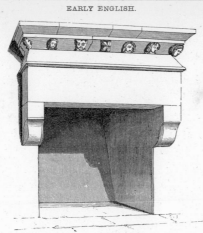

AYDON CASTLE, NORTHUMBERLAND, circa 1270.

DECORATED.

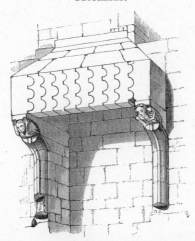

EDLINGHAM CASTLE, NORTHUMBERLAND, circa 1330.

PERPENDICULAR.

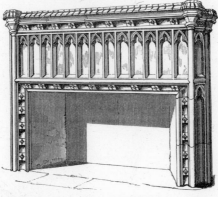

SHERBORNE ABBEY, DORSETSHIRE, circa 1470.

NORMAN

COLESHILL, WARWICKSHIRE,

circa 1150

(The shaft is Decorated)

EARLY ENGLISH.

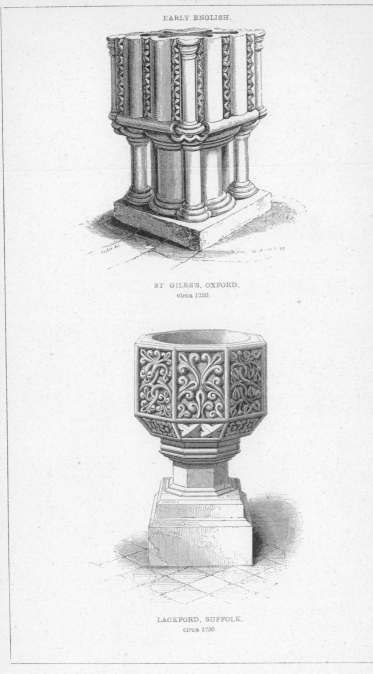

ST GILES'S, OXFORD,
circa 1220.

LACKFORD, SUFFOLK,
circa 1250.

DECORATED.

OFFLEY. HERTFORDSHIRE, c 1350

STANWICK, NORTHAMPTONSHIRE, c. 1350.

PERPENDICULAR

FOTHERINGHAY, NORTHAMPTONSHIRE,
A D   1440

BRADFORD ABBAS, DORSETSHIRE.
circa 1480

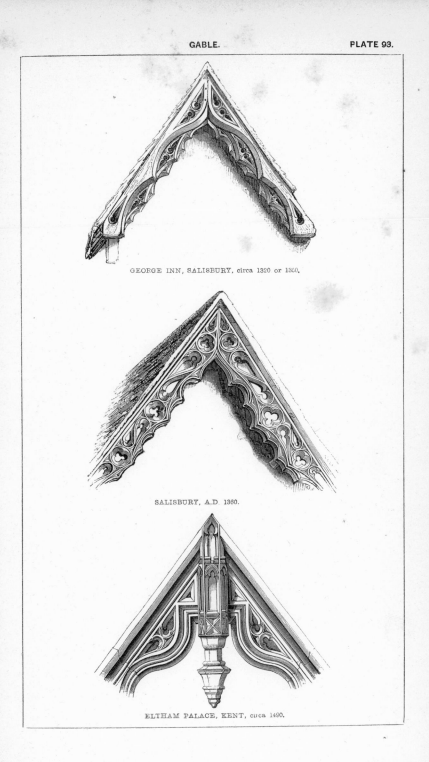

GEORGE INN, SALISBURY, circa 1320 or 1350.

SALISBURY, A.D. 1360.

ELTHAM PALACE, KENT, circa 1490.

DECORATED.

EXETER CATHEDRAL, c. 1300.

FLAMBOYANT.

BURGOS, SPAIN, c. 1500.

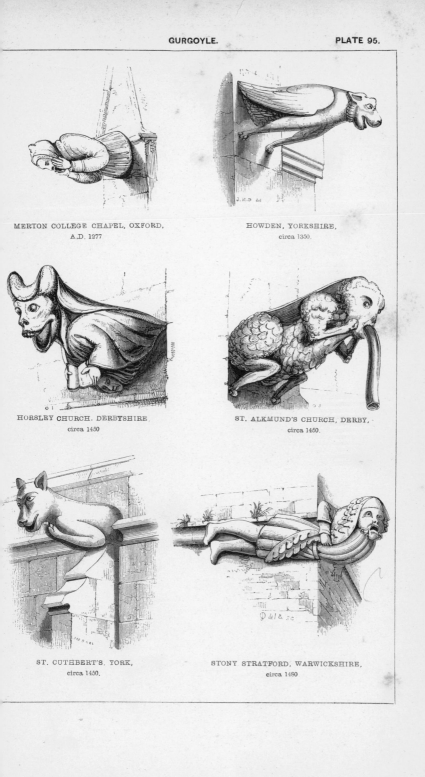

MERTON COLLEGE CHAPEL, OXFORD,
A.D. 1277

HOWDEN, YORKSHIRE,
circa 1350.

HORSLEY CHURCH, DERBYSHIRE,
circa 1450.

ST. ALKMUND'S CHURCH, DERBY,
circa 1450.

ST. CUTHBERT'S, YORK,
circa 1450.

STONY STRATFORD, WARWICKSHIRE,
circa 1480

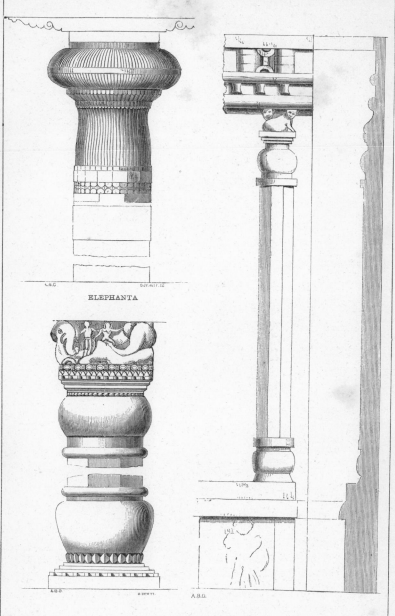

ELEPHANTA

CAVES OF KENNERI, SALSETTE.

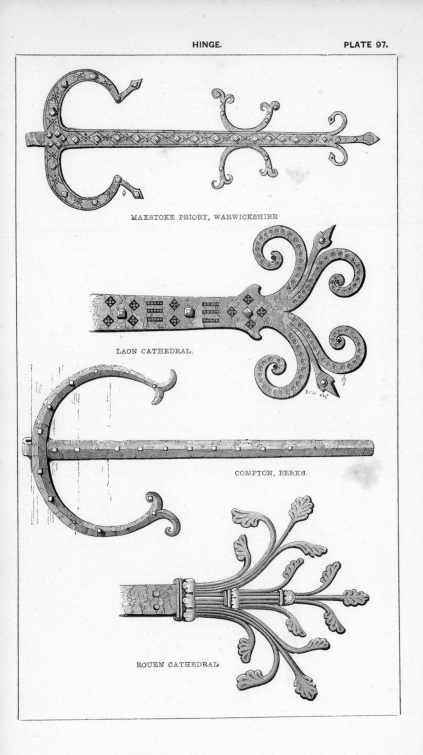

MAXSTOKE PRIORY, WARWICKSHIRE

LAON CATHEDRAL.

COMPTON, BERKS.

ROUEN CATHEDRAL

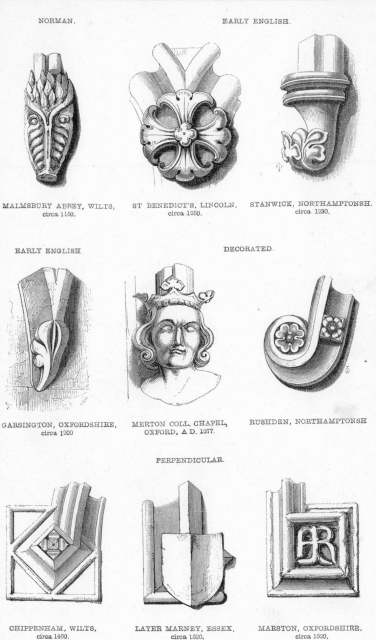

NORMAN.

EARLY ENGLISH.

MALMSBURY ABBEY, WILTS,
circa 1150.

ST BENEDICT'S, LINCOLN,
circa 1250.

STANWICK, NORTHAMPTONSH.
circa 1230.

EARLY ENGLISH

DECORATED.

GARSINGTON, OXFORDSHIRE,
circa 1200

MERTON COLL. CHAPEL,
OXFORD, A.D. 1277.

RUSHDEN, NORTHAMPTONSH.

PERPENDICULAR.

CHIPPENHAM, WILTS,
circa 1460.

LAYER MARNEY, ESSEX,
circa 1520.

MARSTON, OXFORDSHIRE.
circa 1520.

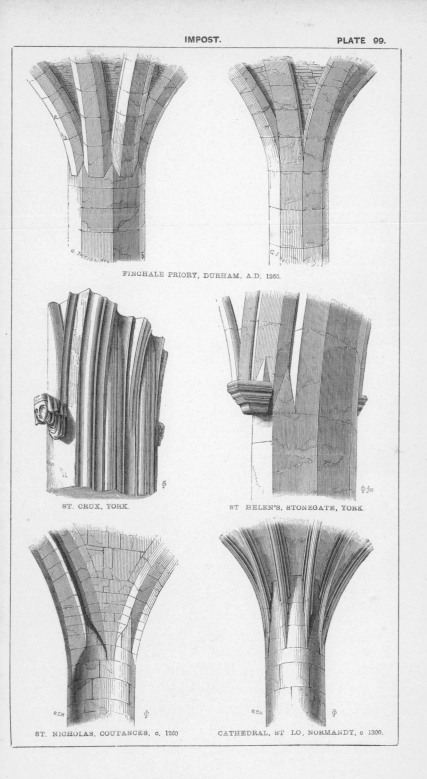

FINCHALE PRIORY, DURHAM, A.D. 1265.

ST. CRUX, YORK.

ST. HELEN'S, STONEGATE, YORK.

ST. NICHOLAS, COUTANCES, c. 1250

CATHEDRAL, ST LO, NORMANDY, c 1300.

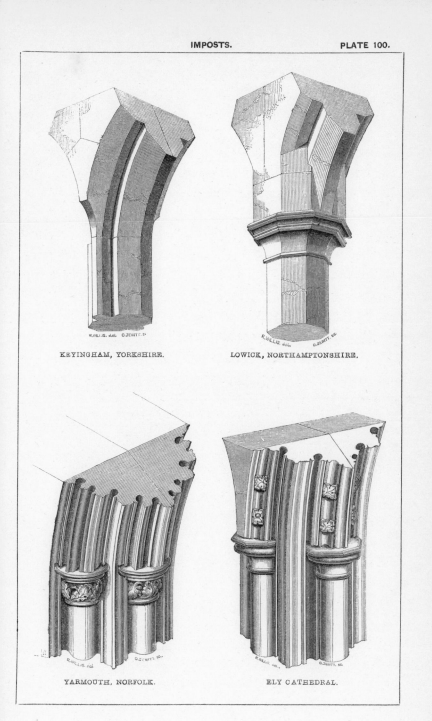

KEYINGHAM, YORKSHIRE.

LOWICK, NORTHAMPTONSHIRE.

YARMOUTH, NORFOLK.

ELY CATHEDRAL.

WINCHESTER CATHEDRAL

MONUMENT OF QUEEN ELEANOR, WESTMINSTER ABBEY, A.D 1294.

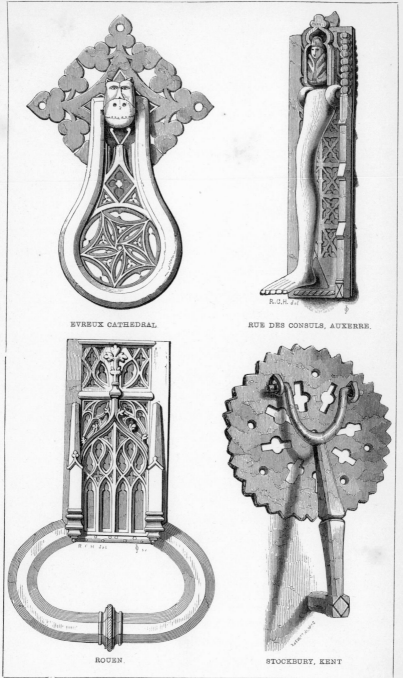

EVREUX CATHEDRAL   RUE DES CONSULS, AUXERRE.

ROUEN.   STOCKBURY, KENT.

CHAPTER-HOUSE, SELBY, YORKSHIRE,
circa 1250.

SALISBURY CATHEDRAL,
circa 1400.

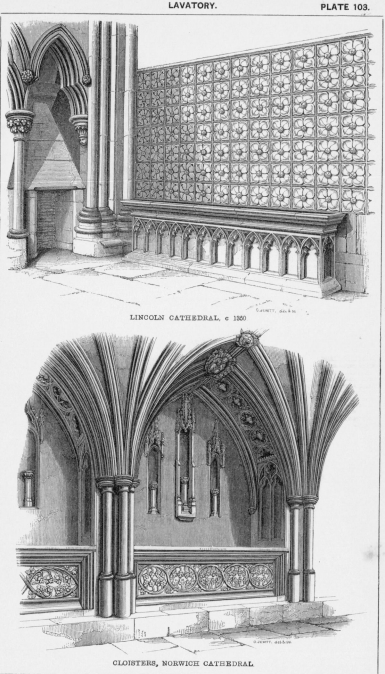

LINCOLN CATHEDRAL, c 1350

CLOISTERS, NORWICH CATHEDRAL.

LETTERNS.

RAMSEY CHURCH, HUNTS. circa 1450.

BURY CHURCH, HUNTS. circa 1300.

FALDSTOOL.

STAINED GLASS, GREAT MALVERN CHURCH

ROUEN CATHEDRAL.

EVREUX. GISORS.

ST GEORGE'S CHAPEL, WINDSOR.

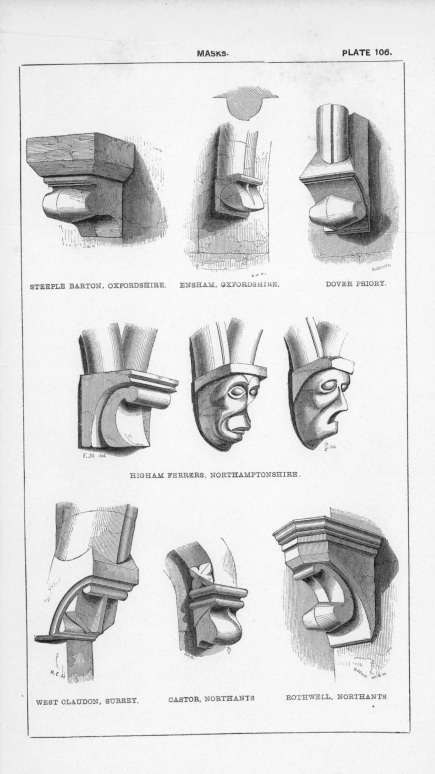

STEEPLE BARTON, OXFORDSHIRE.   ENSHAM, OXFORDSHIRE.   DOVER PRIORY.

HIGHAM FERRERS, NORTHAMPTONSHIRE.

WEST CLAUDON, SURREY.   CASTOR, NORTHANTS   ROTHWELL, NORTHANTS

ROMAN

SOISSONS.   LILLEBONNE.

SILCHESTER   COLCHESTER, ESSEX

MINT WALL, LINCOLN.   PEVENSEY, SUSSEX

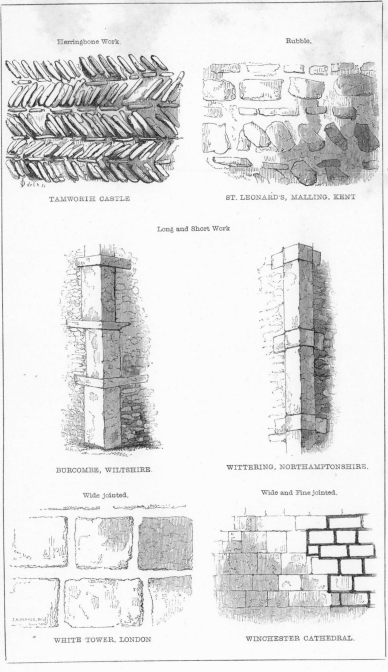

Herringbone Work.   Rubble.

TAMWORTH CASTLE   ST. LEONARD'S, MALLING, KENT.

Long and Short Work

BURCOMBE, WILTSHIRE.   WITTERING, NORTHAMPTONSHIRE.

Wide jointed.   Wide and Fine jointed.

WHITE TOWER, LONDON   WINCHESTER CATHEDRAL.

ENTRANCE TO THE MOSQUE OF CORDOVA, SPAIN

PALACE OF ALHAMBRA, SPAIN.

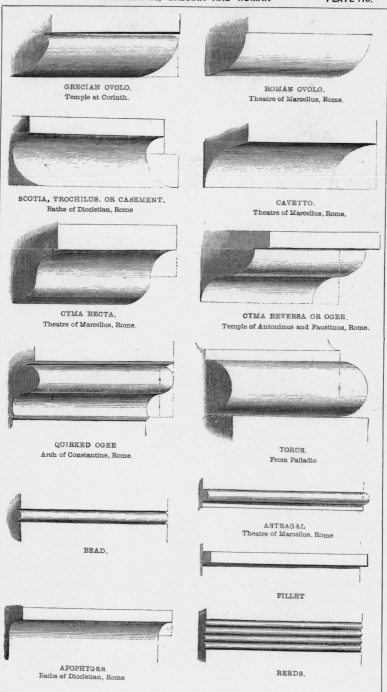

GRECIAN OVOLO.
Temple at Corinth.

ROMAN OVOLO.
Theatre of Marcellus, Rome.

SCOTIA, TROCHILUS, OR CASEMENT.
Baths of Diocletian, Rome

CAVETTO.
Theatre of Marcellus, Rome.

CYMA RECTA.
Theatre of Marcellus, Rome.

CYMA REVERSA OR OGEE.
Temple of Antoninus and Faustinus, Rome.

QUIRKED OGEE
Arch of Constantine, Rome.

TORUS.
From Palladio

BEAD.

ASTRAGAL
Theatre of Marcellus, Rome

FILLET

APOPHYGES.
Baths of Diocletian, Rome

REEDS.

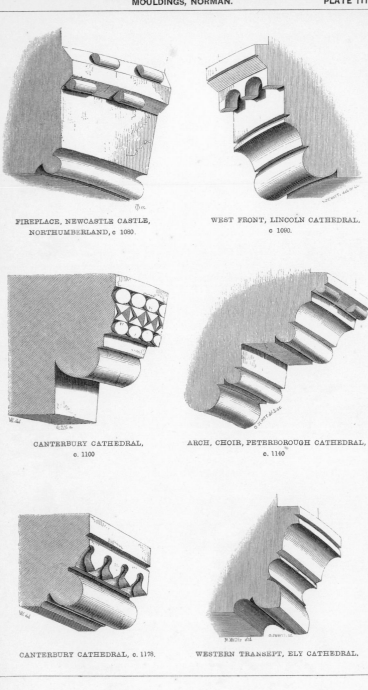

FIREPLACE, NEWCASTLE CASTLE,
NORTHUMBERLAND, c 1080.

WEST FRONT, LINCOLN CATHEDRAL,
c 1090.

CANTERBURY CATHEDRAL,
c. 1100

ARCH, CHOIR, PETERBOROUGH CATHEDRAL,
c. 1140

CANTERBURY CATHEDRAL, c. 1178.

WESTERN TRANSEPT, ELY CATHEDRAL,

NORMAN

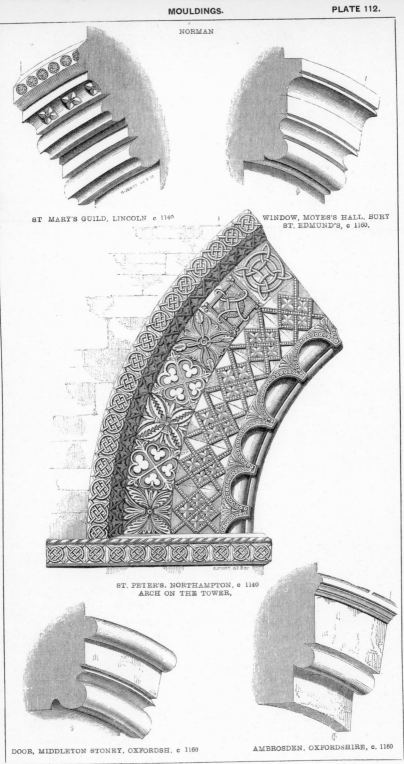

ST MARY'S GUILD, LINCOLN c 1140

WINDOW, MOYES'S HALL, BURY
ST. EDMUND'S, c 1160.

ST. PETER'S, NORTHAMPTON, c 1140
ARCH ON THE TOWER,

DOOR, MIDDLETON STONEY, OXFORDSH. c 1160

AMBROSDEN. OXFORDSHIRE, c. 1160

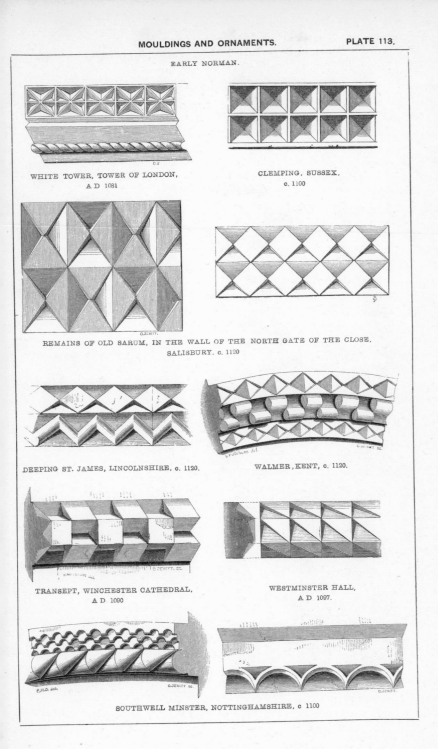

EARLY NORMAN.

WHITE TOWER, TOWER OF LONDON,
A.D 1081

CLEMPING, SUSSEX,
c. 1100

REMAINS OF OLD SARUM, IN THE WALL OF THE NORTH GATE OF THE CLOSE,
SALISBURY, c. 1120

DEEPING ST. JAMES, LINCOLNSHIRE, c. 1120.

WALMER, KENT, c. 1120.

TRANSEPT, WINCHESTER CATHEDRAL,
A.D 1090

WESTMINSTER HALL,
A.D 1097.

SOUTHWELL MINSTER, NOTTINGHAMSHIRE, c 1100

ZIGZAG OR CHEVRON.

NORTH HINKSEY, BERKS

GUIBRAY, NORMANDY

FRESNE CAMILLY, NORMANDY.

BREDGAR, KENT.

WEST DOOR, LINCOLN CATHEDRAL, c. 1140.

NEW ROMNEY, KENT.

IFFLEY, OXFORDSHIRE.

HADISCOE, NORFOLK.

ANDOVER, HANTS

BEAULIEU

Near Caen, Normandy

BARFRESTON, KENT.

SUTTERTON, LINCOLNSHIRE.

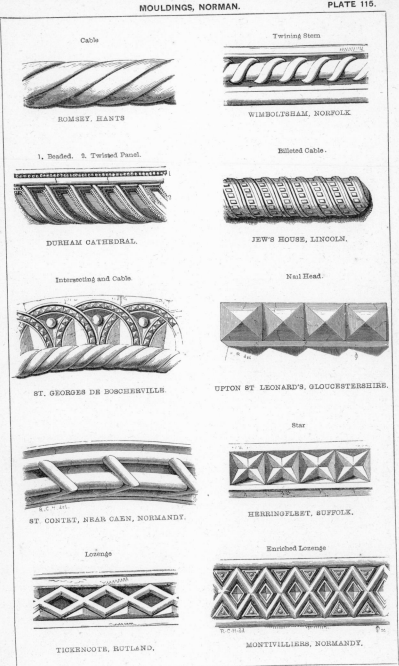

Cable

ROMSEY, HANTS

Twining Stem

WIMBOLTSHAM, NORFOLK

1. Beaded.   2. Twisted Panel.

DURHAM CATHEDRAL.

Billeted Cable.

JEW'S HOUSE, LINCOLN.

Intersecting and Cable.

ST. GEORGES DE BOSCHERVILLE.

Nail Head.

UPTON ST LEONARD'S, GLOUCESTERSHIRE.

ST. CONTET, NEAR CAEN, NORMANDY.

Star

HERRINGFLEET, SUFFOLK.

Lozenge

TICKENCOTE, RUTLAND.

Enriched Lozenge

MONTIVILLIERS, NORMANDY.

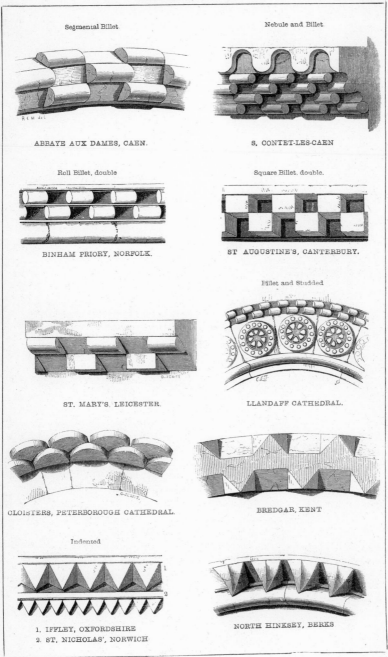

Segmental Billet

ABBAYE AUX DAMES, CAEN.

Nebule and Billet.

S. CONTET-LES-CAEN

Roll Billet, double

BINHAM PRIORY, NORFOLK.

Square Billet, double.

ST AUGUSTINE'S, CANTERBURY.

ST. MARY'S, LEICESTER.

Billet and Studded

LLANDAFF CATHEDRAL.

CLOISTERS, PETERBOROUGH CATHEDRAL.

BREDGAR, KENT

Indented

1. IFFLEY, OXFORDSHIRE
2. ST. NICHOLAS', NORWICH

NORTH HINKSEY, BERKS

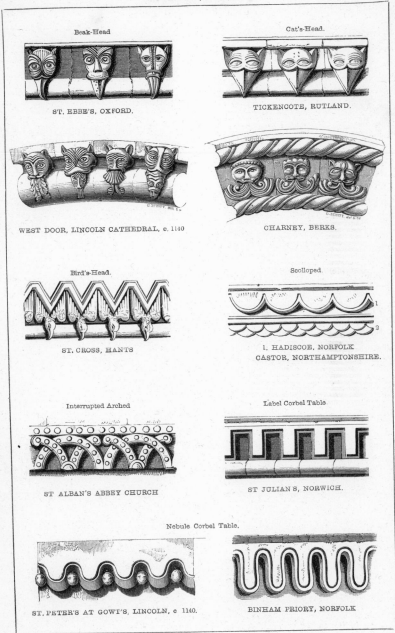

Beak-Head

ST. EBBE'S, OXFORD.

Cat's-Head.

TICKENCOTE, RUTLAND.

WEST DOOR, LINCOLN CATHEDRAL, c. 1140

CHARNEY, BERKS.

Bird's-Head.

ST. CROSS, HANTS

Scolloped.

1. HADISCOE, NORFOLK
CASTOR, NORTHAMPTONSHIRE.

Interrupted Arched

ST ALBAN'S ABBEY CHURCH

Label Corbel Table.

ST JULIAN'S, NORWICH.

Nebule Corbel Table.

ST. PETER'S AT GOWT'S, LINCOLN, c 1140.

BINHAM PRIORY, NORFOLK

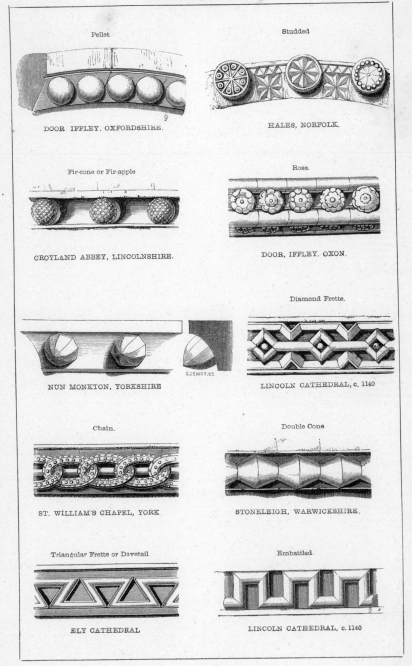

Pellet

DOOR IFFLEY, OXFORDSHIRE.

Studded

HALES, NORFOLK.

Fir-cone or Fir-apple

CROYLAND ABBEY, LINCOLNSHIRE.

Rose.

DOOR, IFFLEY. OXON.

NUN MONKTON, YORKSHIRE

Diamond Frette.

LINCOLN CATHEDRAL, c. 1140

Chain.

ST. WILLIAM'S CHAPEL, YORK

Double Cone

STONELEIGH, WARWICKSHIRE.

Triangular Frette or Dovetail.

ELY CATHEDRAL

Embattled.

LINCOLN CATHEDRAL, c. 1140

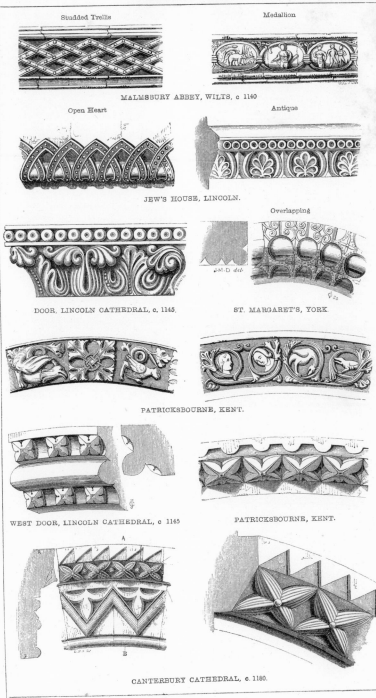

Studded Trellis

Medallion

MALMSBURY ABBEY, WILTS, c 1140

Open Heart

Antique

JEW'S HOUSE, LINCOLN.

DOOR, LINCOLN CATHEDRAL, c. 1145.

Overlapping

J.M.D del

ST. MARGARET'S, YORK.

PATRICKSBOURNE, KENT.

WEST DOOR, LINCOLN CATHEDRAL, c 1145

PATRICKSBOURNE, KENT.

A

B

CANTERBURY CATHEDRAL, c. 1180.

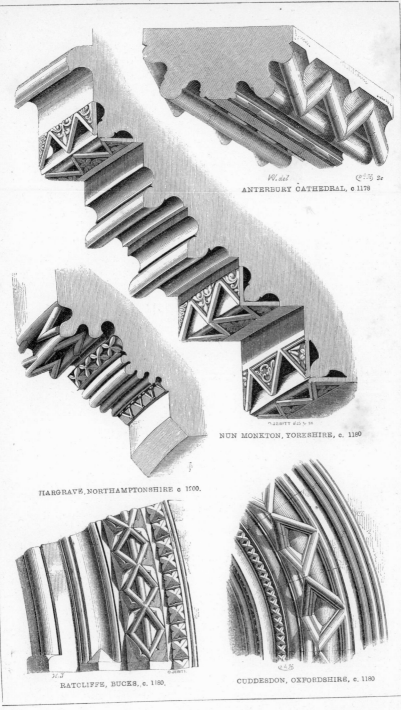

ANTERBURY CATHEDRAL, c 1178

NUN MONKTON, YORKSHIRE, c. 1180

HARGRAVE, NORTHAMPTONSHIRE c 1200.

RATCLIFFE, BUCKS, c. 1180.

CUDDESDON, OXFORDSHIRE, c. 1180

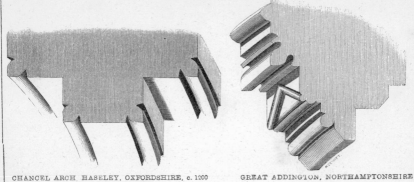

CHANCEL ARCH, HASELEY, OXFORDSHIRE, c. 1200

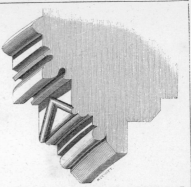

GREAT ADDINGTON, NORTHAMPTONSHIRE

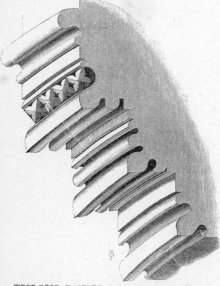

WEST DOOR, HASELEY, OXFORDSHIRE, c. 1200

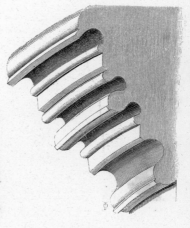

COURTLODGE, GODMERSHAM, KENT, c. 1260.

NETLEY ABBEY, circa 1260.

NORTH DOOR, KIDLINGTON, OXON, c. 1250.

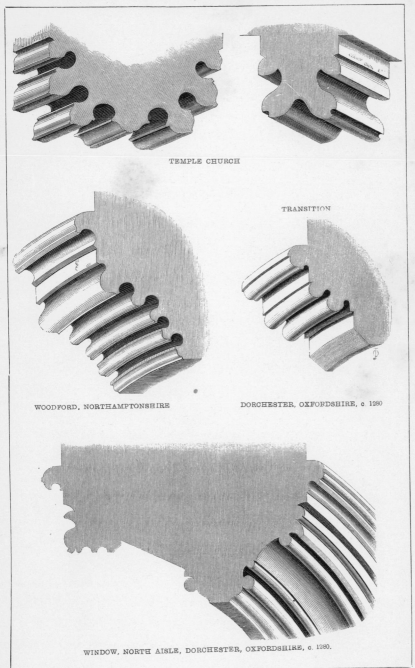

TEMPLE CHURCH

TRANSITION

WOODFORD, NORTHAMPTONSHIRE   DORCHESTER, OXFORDSHIRE, c. 1280

WINDOW, NORTH AISLE, DORCHESTER, OXFORDSHIRE, c. 1280.

TOOTH ORNAMENT.

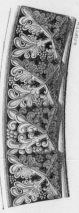

LINCOLN CATHEDRAL.   CHIPPING WARDEN,   PETERBOROUGH   STONE, KENT
                     NORTHAMPTONSH.   CATHEDRAL.

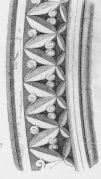

BINHAM PRIORY, NORFOLK

DUNSTABLE PRIORY.   WEST DOOR, ST CROSS, HANTS.

DECORATED.

SOUTHWELL MINSTER, NOTTS.   CHERRINGTON, WARWICKSHIRE

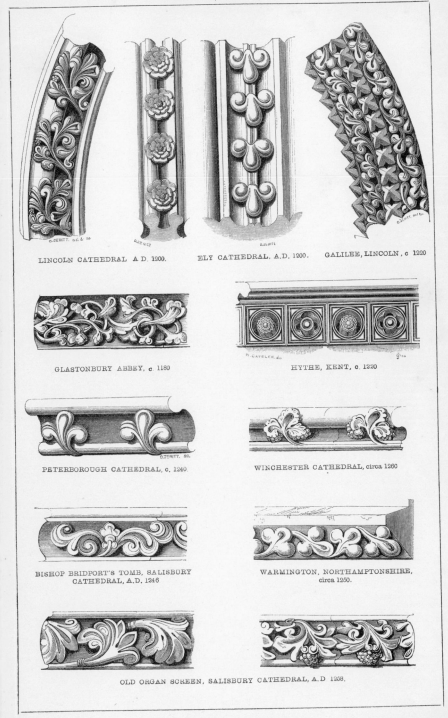

LINCOLN CATHEDRAL A D. 1200.   ELY CATHEDRAL, A.D. 1200.   GALILEE, LINCOLN, c 1220

GLASTONBURY ABBEY, c. 1180   HYTHE, KENT, c. 1220

PETERBOROUGH CATHEDRAL, c. 1240.   WINCHESTER CATHEDRAL, circa 1260

BISHOP BRIDPORT'S TOMB, SALISBURY
CATHEDRAL, A.D. 1246   WARMINGTON, NORTHAMPTONSHIRE,
circa 1250.

OLD ORGAN SCREEN, SALISBURY CATHEDRAL, A.D 1258.

DECORATED

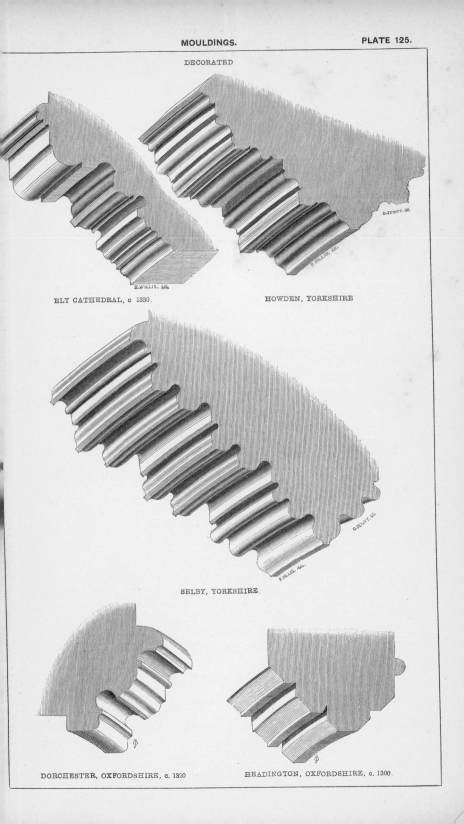

ELY CATHEDRAL, c 1330.

HOWDEN, YORKSHIRE

SELBY, YORKSHIRE.

DORCHESTER, OXFORDSHIRE, c. 1320

HEADINGTON, OXFORDSHIRE, c. 1300.

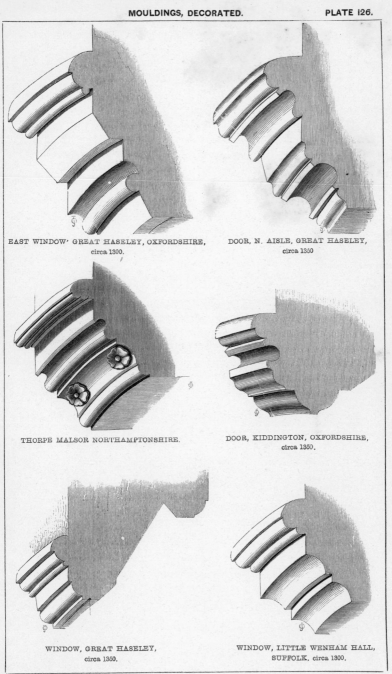

EAST WINDOW GREAT HASELEY, OXFORDSHIRE,
circa 1300.

DOOR, N. AISLE, GREAT HASELEY,
circa 1350

THORPE MALSOR NORTHAMPTONSHIRE.

DOOR, KIDDINGTON, OXFORDSHIRE,
circa 1350.

WINDOW, GREAT HASELEY,
circa 1350.

WINDOW, LITTLE WENHAM HALL,
SUFFOLK, circa 1300.

DECORATED.

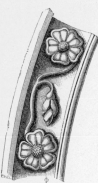

HAWTON, NOTTS,
c. 1300

WEST DOOR, YORK
CATHEDRAL, c. 1350.

SOUTHWELL MINSTER.
NOTTS, c. 1300

WELLINGBOROUGH,
NORTHAMPTONSHIRE, c. 1300

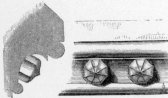

ST MARY'S, BEVERLEY, c 1300.

DOOR, ADDERBURY, OXON, c 1330

SOUTHWELL MINSTER, NOTTS, c 1300.

LADY CHAPEL, WELLS CATHEDRAL, c. 1330

Four-leaved Flower

NORTH WINDOW, COGGS, OXON, c. 1350.

LATIN CHAPEL, OXFORD CATHEDRAL, c. 1350.

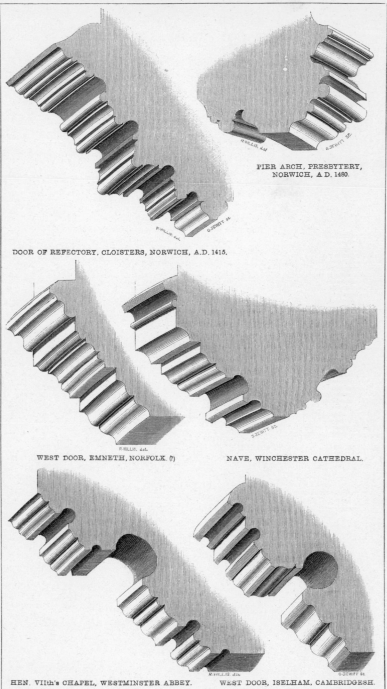

PIER ARCH, PRESBYTERY,
NORWICH, A.D. 1480.

DOOR OF REFECTORY, CLOISTERS, NORWICH, A.D. 1415.

WEST DOOR, EMNETH, NORFOLK. (?)   NAVE, WINCHESTER CATHEDRAL.

HEN. VIIth's CHAPEL, WESTMINSTER ABBEY.   WEST DOOR, ISELHAM, CAMBRIDGESH.

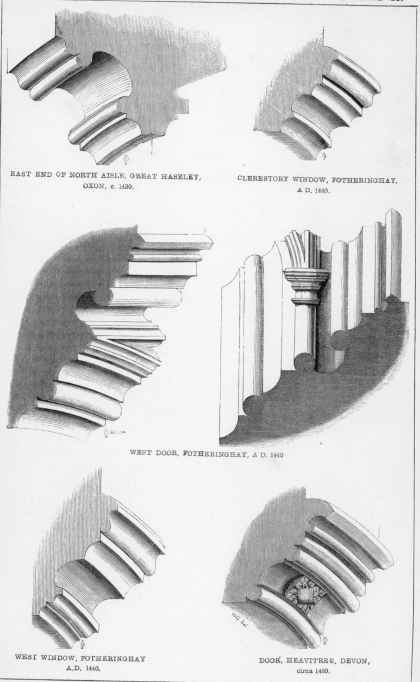

EAST END OF NORTH AISLE, GREAT HASELEY,
OXON, c. 1430.

CLERESTORY WINDOW, FOTHERINGHAY,
A D. 1440.

WEST DOOR, FOTHERINGHAY, A D. 1440

WEST WINDOW, FOTHERINGHAY
A.D. 1440.

DOOR, HEAVITREE, DEVON,
circa 1480.

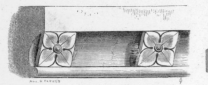

PORLOCK, SOMERSETSHIRE
circa 1460.

OPEN SEAT, COMBE IN TEIGNHEAD,
DEVONSHIRE, c 1500.

MONUMENT, WELLS CATHEDRAL, A.D. 1465.

ST. ALBAN'S, HERTFORDSHIRE, A.D. 1447.

ST FRIDESWIDE'S SHRINE, OXFORD CATHEDRAL, circa 1480

WHITCHURCH, SOMERSETSHIRE,
circa 1480.

ST ALBAN'S, HERTFORDSHIRE,
circa 1480.

WEST END OF NAVE, ST. MARY'S,
OXFORD, A.D. 1488.

HENRY VII CHAPEL, WESTMINSTER
A.D. 1510.

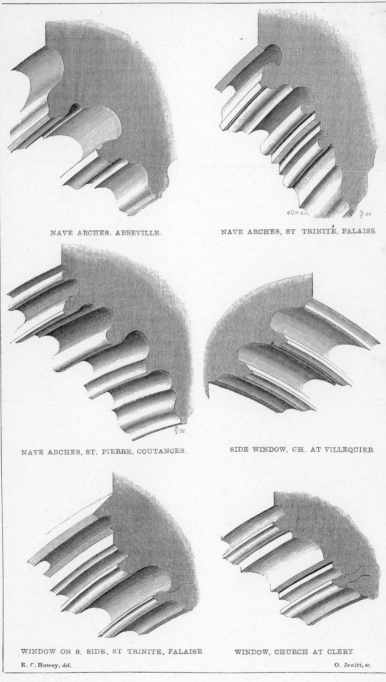

NAVE ARCHES, ABBEVILLE.

NAVE ARCHES, ST TRINITÉ, FALAISE.

NAVE ARCHES, ST. PIERRE, COUTANCES.

SIDE WINDOW, CH. AT VILLEQUIER.

WINDOW ON S. SIDE, ST TRINITE, FALAISE

WINDOW, CHURCH AT CLERY.

R. C. Hussey, *del.*

O. Jewitt, *sc.*

BASEMENTS.

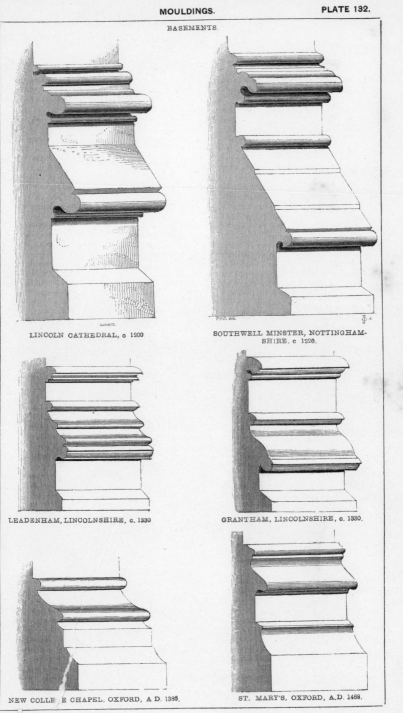

LINCOLN CATHEDRAL, c 1200

SOUTHWELL MINSTER, NOTTINGHAM-
SHIRE. c 1220.

LEADENHAM, LINCOLNSHIRE, c. 1330

GRANTHAM, LINCOLNSHIRE, c. 1330.

NEW COLLEGE CHAPEL, OXFORD, A.D. 1386.

ST. MARY'S, OXFORD, A.D. 1488.

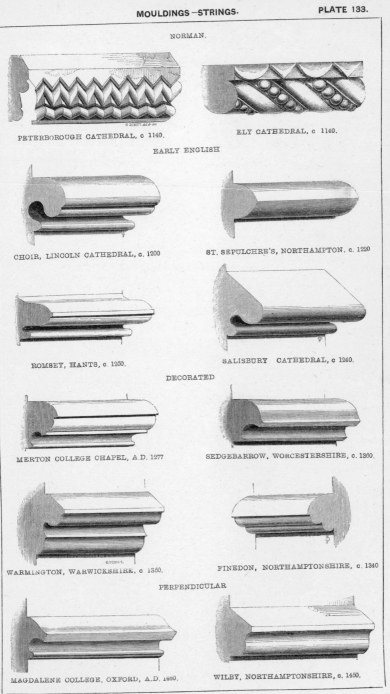

NORMAN.

PETERBOROUGH CATHEDRAL, c 1140.

ELY CATHEDRAL, c 1140.

EARLY ENGLISH

CHOIR, LINCOLN CATHEDRAL, c. 1200

ST. SEPULCHRE'S, NORTHAMPTON. c. 1220

ROMSEY, HANTS, c. 1250.

SALISBURY CATHEDRAL, c 1240.

DECORATED

MERTON COLLEGE CHAPEL, A.D. 1277

SEDGEBARROW, WORCESTERSHIRE, c. 1360.

WARMINGTON, WARWICKSHIRE, c 1350.

FINEDON, NORTHAMPTONSHIRE, c. 1340

PERPENDICULAR

MAGDALENE COLLEGE, OXFORD, A.D. 1480.

WILBY, NORTHAMPTONSHIRE, c. 1450.

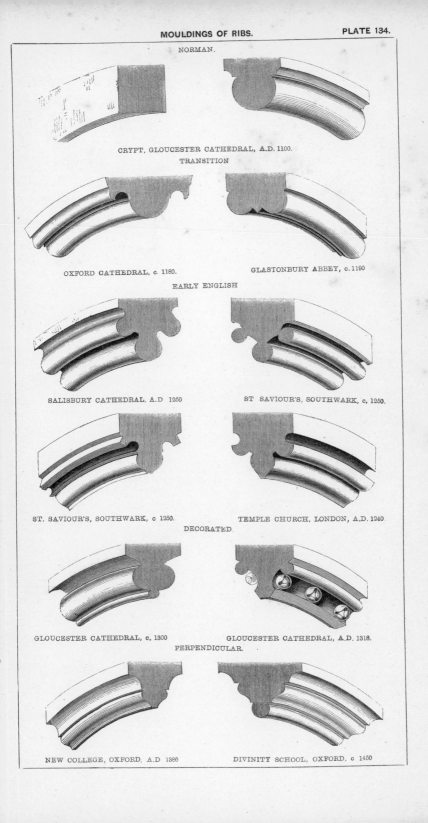

NORMAN.

CRYPT, GLOUCESTER CATHEDRAL, A.D. 1100.

TRANSITION

OXFORD CATHEDRAL, c. 1180.   GLASTONBURY ABBEY, c. 1190.

EARLY ENGLISH

SALISBURY CATHEDRAL, A.D 1250   ST SAVIOUR'S, SOUTHWARK, c. 1250.

ST. SAVIOUR'S, SOUTHWARK, c 1250.   TEMPLE CHURCH, LONDON, A.D. 1240.

DECORATED.

GLOUCESTER CATHEDRAL, c. 1300   GLOUCESTER CATHEDRAL, A.D. 1318.

PERPENDICULAR.

NEW COLLEGE, OXFORD, A.D 1386   DIVINITY SCHOOL, OXFORD, c 1450

WARMINGTON, NORTHANTS   WESTMINSTER ABBEY.   SALISBURY CATHEDRAL.

ROTHWELL, NORTHANTS.   CANTERBURY CATHEDRAL.   FINEDON, NORTHANTS.

BAYHAM ABBEY, SUSSEX   PITSFORD, NORTHANTS   FINEDON, NORTHANTS.

EARLY ENGLISH.

DECORATED.

SPIRE, WITNEY, OXON, c. 1250

SPIRE, ST. MARY'S, OXFORD, c. 1280.

CHOIR, MERTON COLL CHAPEL, A D 1277.

ST. MICHAEL'S, OXFORD, c. 1300.

DECORATED.

PERPENDICULAR.

OXFORD CATHEDRAL

TEWKESBURY, c. 1320.

OXFORD CATHEDRAL, c. 1320.

OXFORD CATHEDRAL, c. 1355.

WESTMINSTER HALL, c. 1380

PERPENDICULAR.

NEW COLL CHAPEL, OXFORD, A.D. 1386.

MERTON COLL. CHAPEL. A.D. 1424.

LINCOLN CATHEDRAL, c. 1450

BURFORD, OXON, c 1500.